THE HUMOR
OF THE
AMERICAN COWBOY

He let that poor ol' hoss come home all by itself

The Humor
of the
American Cowboy

By
STAN HOIG

ILLUSTRATED BY NICK EGGENHOFER

UNIVERSITY OF NEBRASKA PRESS · LINCOLN

In memory of my father,
MELVIN E. HOIG

Preface

THIS BOOK is a direct result of the admiration I
hold for the American cowboy. Having been born
and reared in a cattle-raising area of the Southwest, I have known many cowboys and cattlemen.
I once spent one of my more enjoyable autumns
in a line shack with a rheumatism-stove cow poke
named Bill, whose major misery in life was bed-
bugs. As far as I know, Bill never took any action
against them except to complain once in a while.

I am especially grateful to those cow hands who
braved the deserts of rhetoric to report their part

of cowboy life. In collecting this material on the American cowboy and his humor, I have read scores of books written by cowboys who wanted to give a true account of cowboy life as it was in the old days.

While I have tried to point out a few of the relevant facts concerning the cowboy's personality, my aim has largely been to pass on the cowboy's humor for the entertainment and enlightenment of the uninitiated. Most of these jokes and stories are old mossybacks and have been around a-plenty. But for those not overly familiar with the Old West, this humor should be just as fresh as it was when a man could ride a hundred miles and never see a fence. The biggest part of the gather has been rounded up from the back-brush of libraries. Some are a little woolly, but I'm sure that whoever sinks his teeth into this beef will agree that it's salty!

I am deeply obligated to Mr. Brent Ashabranner, who offered invaluable roundup assistance; to Dr. Cecil B. Williams, of Oklahoma State University, without whose friendly interest and chuck-wagon advice these longhorns might never have made a herd; and to my wife Pat who took on the chore of loading these critters. I am grateful, also, to Dr. E. E. Dale and to Ramon F. Adams for their kind encouragement.

I also wish to thank *American Mercury* for permission to reprint "The Windy West," which appeared in their October, 1953, issue, and *Railroad Magazine* for permission to reprint "Cowboy *vs.* Railroader," which appeared in their December, 1953, issue.

And my thanks to Bill for some of the finest complaining I have ever heard!

Table of Contents

List of Illustrations

THE HUMOR
OF THE
AMERICAN COWBOY

Chapter I

Laugh Kills Lonesome

*"To understand ranch lingo all yuh
have to do is to know in advance what
the other feller means an' then pay
no attention to what he says."*[1]

THE OLD WILD WEST is gone. The sands of time
drift thicker and thicker over the days of the open
range, of great cattle herds, of reckless, free-riding
men on horseback. The physical existence of the
Old West is recalled only by a deserted trail

---

[1] Philip Ashton Rollins, *The Cowboy; His Characteristics, His
Equipment, and His Part in the Development of the West* (Reprint ed.; New York: Charles Scribner's Sons, 1936), p. 237.

town, a crumbling adobe wall, a stretch of tram-
pled ground that was once a boulevard of cattle
traffic. Only a scant few of the old cowboy breed
remain, gnarled old-timers whose memories are
filled with lore of the past. To these remnants
of the cowboy legion, the ghosts of yesterday
beckon as they gallop with the sweeping prairie
winds.

More than half a century has passed since the
cowboy empire began its decline. It left behind
no architectural monuments; the trees of science
and religion bore no fruit for posterity. Even
the social development of the West was made
largely *in spite of* the cattle industry. Yet the
cowboy era had a greatness about it, a greatness
of spirit that was as much a part of the cowboy
as the cowboy was a part of his times. It was a
spirit of strong men in a free world, based on a
combination of physical and psychological stam-
ina. Out of it grew an understanding of human
nature and a realistic attitude toward life that
was expressed in rich, fertile humor.

Will Rogers, whose wit and sagebrush philosophy caught the fancy of the world, was a product
of the cowboy's humor. Though Rogers' scope
of thought ranged far wider than did that of the
ordinary cow poke, his humor has roots that sink
deep into the cow country.

But this real glory that was the cowboy's appears destined for oblivion. The chief consequence of the cowboy's brief hour upon the stage has been to furnish a character type for modern entertainment media. The romance and adventure attached to his person offer excellent opportunities for commercialization. In the many billions of words that have been written about the cowboy, scant attention has been paid to his amazing capacity for humor. As a result the true image of the cowboy rides a lonely trail today, its saddle mates few, the ambushers many. Historical reality is sinking into a quagmire of rodeo costumes, hillbilly singers, and television and movie heroes.

Even the folklorists have become so fascinated with the cowboy that they have ordained a folk hero for him. When Pecos Bill appeared in a 1923 *Century Magazine* article, he was accepted, evidently without question, as a rival for Paul Bunyan, Febold Feboldson, and folk heroes of other areas. Since then, the students of Western folklore have continued to attribute the tall tales of the range to the Pecos Bill myth.[2]

In 1919, four years prior to the *Century* article, John A. Lomax published his *Songs of the Cattle*

---

[2] Brent Ashabranner, "Pecos Bill—An Appraisal," *Western Folklore*, Vol. XI (December, 1948). This article pretty well explodes the theory of Pecos Bill as a real cow-camp folk hero.

Trail and Cow Camp. It contains a reading entitled "The Legend of Boastful Bill." This verse appears to be at least one bona fide ancestor of the Pecos Bill yarns.

THE LEGEND OF BOASTFUL BILL

At a roundup on the Gila
One sweet morning long ago,
Ten of us was throwed quite freely
By a hoss from Idaho.
An' we 'lowed he'd go a-beggin'
For a man to break his pride
Till, a-hitchin' up one leggin',
Boastful Bill cut loose an' cried:
  "I'm a ornery proposition for to hurt,
  I fulfill my earthly mission with a quirt,
  I can ride the highest liver
  'Twixt the Gulf an' Powder River,
  An' I'll break this thing as easy as I'd flirt."

So Bill climbed the Northern fury
An' they mangled up the air
Till a native of Missouri
Would have owned the brag was fair.
Though the plunges kept him reelin'
An' the wind it flapped his shirt,
Loud above the hoss's squealin'
We could hear our friend assert:
  "I'm the one to take such rockin' as a joke;
  Someone hand me up the makin' of a smoke.
  If you think my fame needs brightnin',
  Why, I'll rope a streak o' lightnin'
  An' spur it up an' quirt it till it's broke."

Then one caper of repulsion
Broke that hoss's back in two,
Cinches snapped in the convulsion,
Skyward man and saddle flew,
Up they mounted, never flaggin',
And we watched them through our tears,
While this last, thin bit o' braggin'
Came a-floatin' to our ears:
    "If you ever watched my habits very close,
    You would know I broke such rabbits by the gross.
    I have kept my talent hidin',
    I'm too good for earthly ridin',
    So I'm off to bust the lightnin'—Adios!"

Years have passed since that ascension;
Boastful Bill ain't never lit;
So we reckon he's a-wrenchin'
Some celestial outlaw's bit.
When the night wind flaps our slickers,
And the rain is cold and stout,
And the lightnin' flares and flickers,
We can sometimes hear him shout:
    "I'm a-ridin' son o' thunder o' the sky,
    I'm a broncho twistin' wonder on the fly.
    Hey, you earthlin's, shut your winders,
    We're a-rippin' clouds to flinders.
    If this blue-eyed darlin' kicks at you, you die."

Star-dust on his chaps and saddle,
Scornful still of jar and jolt,
He'll come back sometime a-straddle
Of a bald-faced thunderbolt;
And the thin-skinned generation
Of that dim and distant day
Sure will stare with admiration
When they hear old Boastful say:

"I was first, as old raw-hiders all confest,
I'm the last of all rough riders, and the best.
Huh! you soft and dainty floaters
With your aeroplanes and motors,
Huh! are you the greatgrandchildren of the West?"

From recitation, original, by CHARLES·
BADGER CLARK, JR.[3]

To bundle the cowboy's humor into one legendary character such as Pecos Bill is to report him falsely. The type of yarn where a super cowboy does super deeds is a weak sister to the versatile, hair-on-its-chest humor of the range. In the first place the cowboy was much too individualistic to accept a standard figure for his humor; and, secondly, his imagination far surpassed any such single creation. Thirdly, range humor, which by no means limited itself to the tall-tale form, grew mostly out of real, everyday happenings. Even the most fantastic tall story was based on some elemental fact of cowboy life.

The cowboy's humor is extremely revealing of him for it reflects his pastimes, his pleasures, his complaints, his reactions to the circus of creation that even in its tragic moments seemed to hold some amusement for him. The cowboy may have realized instinctively that he was a mammal soon

---

[3] Charles Badger Clark, Jr. (ed.), in *Sun and Saddle Leather* (New ed.; Boston: R. G. Badger [c. 1917]), as reprinted by John A. Lomax (comp.), *Songs of the Cattle Trail and Cow Camp* (First ed.; New York: The Macmillan Company, 1919), p. 8.

to lose out in the upheavals of social order. Songs such as "The Cowboy's Lament" reflect that he sensed the fate which awaited his breed. Yet there was in him such supreme devotion and pride for his way of life that he would have chosen no other trail to ride.

Someone once described the cowboy as a "man with guts and a hoss," but whoever said it didn't do the cowboy justice. To describe the cowboy truthfully, the definition would be more apt to read, "a man with guts and a hoss and a heck uv a sense of humor." This last best marks him for what he was.

Without his humor, it is doubtful that the cowboy could have survived, for his knack for seeing the humorous side of life was every bit as vital to him as his rope, horse, or six gun. Without an ability to laugh at troubles and hard times, the cowboy could never have withstood the pressures piled on him in a world of strenuous work and violent action. It was typical of a cowboy who had been put afoot by a rabbit-shy cayuse to respond by shaking his fist after the animal and declaring, "Jes' fer that, I'm gonna walk home!" And when the waddie trudged, footsore and weary, back into ranch headquarters, he would likely be asked what in the heck he meant by making that poor animal come home all by itself. The man who felt sorry for himself out West was lost.

Moreover, a healthy sense of humor was often the best solution to many range problems. While on roundup once, the foreman of an outfit found that his crew was blessed with a chronic grumbler. This particular waddie never liked the camping place the cook had chosen nor the food he fixed and was constantly complaining about one thing or another. Wanting to keep harmony, the foreman took this in silence for some time, but finally he could stand it no longer. One day the cowboy came to him with a complaint about the food, and the foreman told him that there was nothing wrong with the food, that what he needed was some "liver-regulator." He suggested that the cook might be able to supply him with some of the medicine, which was kept in the grub box. Others of the crew took up the suggestion and urged the cowboy to try some of the cook's remedy.

Finally, after complaining his way through a meal, the grumbler walked up to the cookie and said, "Say, how about some of that liver-regulator they been tellin' me about? I hope it's better than the meals we been gettin'."

The cook looked him over.

"It sure is," he agreed and reached into the

This is the best darned liver regulator
I know about.

grub box. His hand came out with a cocked .45 in it.

"This is the best darned liver regulator I know about," the cookie said. "An' if I hear one more word outa you, I'm gonna let you have a big dose of it."

The improvement in the waddie's health was remarkable.[4]

On another occasion there was a big, overgrown cow poke named Tall Cotton, whose speciality was going to sleep during duty hours, leaving the rest of the crew to do his share of the work. The boys took it for a time, but they finally decided that something had to be done about the matter.

Then came the day they found Cotton curled up in a haystack, boots off, sound asleep. The opportunity was golden. The boys rounded up a huge tarantula, killed it, and laid it close to Cotton's leg. Then they tied a pin on the end of a stick and jabbed the sleeping waddie a couple of times. Cotton came awake like a wild Comanche doing the snake dance and, at the same time, a cowboy rushed up and smashed the tarantula with his boot heel.

---

4 Lewis Nordyke, *Cattle Empire; The Fabulous Story of the 3,000,000 Acre XIT* (New York: William Morrow & Company, Inc., 1949), pp. 140-41.

Cotton took one look at the dead tarantula and turned white. He began to get sick, even though the other waddies did their best to console him with stories of the horrible deaths they had seen as a result of tarantula bites. Finally, one of the crew, who laid claim to having read *Ten Thousand Things Worth Knowing,* as well as *Dr. Chase's Recipe Book,* offered to try to save Cotton, even though he admitted it seemed hopeless.

First the cowboy poured a pint of bear's oil down Cotton. When that started some of the poison coming out of him, they followed it up with a glass of soda, a cup of vinegar, and finally a quart of water in which a plug of tobacco had been soaking. For a while it seemed almost certain that Cotton was going to die from that tarantula bite; but the medicine was potent and, eventually, he was saved. After that, the crew had very little trouble with him lying down on the job, especially in haystacks.[5]

The ability to laugh off a serious matter saved as many cowboy hides as the six gun ever did. There was, for instance, the trail herder who hit town and refused to take his turn at standing

---

[5] John James Callison, *Bill Jones of Paradise Valley, Oklahoma; His Life and Adventures for Over Forty Years in the Great South-west* [Chicago, Printed by M. A. Donohue & Co., c. 1914], p. 112.

guard on the herd. The trail boss went after him and found the cowboy with a ripsnorting drunk in progress. When the boss demanded that the cowboy return to the herd, the other announced that he wouldn't stand guard that night for any man, including General Grant. The trail boss saw that argument was going to accomplish little. He knocked the cowboy down, whereupon the man got up; whereupon the boss knocked him down again. After hitting the ground for the third time, the waddie shook his head and looked up at the trail boss who towered over him.

"Boss," he asked with a sheepish grin, "jes' which way did you say that ol' herd was?"[6]

Humor was even more vital to the cow country as a source of entertainment and relaxation. After long hours in the saddle, cowboys had to have some sort of release from the strain and fatigue. Tall-tale sessions, joking, pranking, and storytelling were often the results.

"I reckon we'll have to try Slim Watkins this afternoon fur onbecomin' misdemeanors," drawled the wagon boss.
Slim was gone and therefore oblivious of the situation that faced him.

---

[6] Frank M. King, *Wranglin' the Past* (Pasadena, Calif.: Trail's End Publishing Co., 1935), p. 109.

"For what will you arrest him?" asked the cook.

"Oh, say fur brandin' a maverick fur that red-headed female in Trinidad."

"He'll be hard to catch if he knows."

"Oh, no he won't. I'll git him when he comes in."

Spring roundup of 1887, camped on the Ute Creek, NE New Mexico. Cowboys "lying over" must have diversion, and one of the never tiring amusements such situations provided is a mock trial. The sentences imposed by the "court" are various and as severe as the "Judge" can invent.

"Will be lots of wild plums here this summer," Slim remarks as he got off his horse, "that is, if the hail don't hit 'em."

"Will be gone by beef hunt time," argued an innocent bystander.

The cowboys eat and after supper Slim is grabbed.

"Slim," said the functionary, "yer goin' ter trial."

A sheriff and two attorneys are delegated to their respective tasks. Denied a jury, the accused stands before the judge who sits on a wagon tongue and whittles.

"Proceed with this yere case."

The "attorney" for the prosecution was the first to speak. "This puncher what yer all knows is Slim Watkins. He's sure ornery, which yer likewise knows of. He'd turn a day herd loose if he dared, an' beats his horse over the head with his quirt. He's before yer as havin' branded a big yearlin' calf fur a girl named Em, which lives in Trinidad, an' is red-headed an' plain."

"Any evidence?" inquired the judge.

"Reckon so. Yer knows her, don't yer?"

"I mean as ter the brandin'," said the court as all laughed at his expense.

The trial proceeds and witnesses testify. One claims he caught Slim in the act of placing a brand on a white-faced calf; that the animal was hog-tied, a fire of bull chips had been built on the prairie, and that the prisoner was marking the calf "EM on the left side an' swallerfork both ears which he said was fer 'Em.' "

Other character witnesses testified Slim "had beaten a widow out of a wash bill, stolen a new rope from a tenderfoot, and put a dead rattlesnake in the range manager's bed."

The attorney for the defense claimed in rebuttal, "This 'ere is a frame-up."

But Slim was adjudged "guilty" and "considering the unusual orneryness of the offense" to be thrown into the water-hole near camp in his clothes, hat, spurs, and boots. He was to be closely watched and no attempt made to rescue him if he sank. On reaching shore he was to be stripped of his pants, laid over the wagon tongue, to receive a dozen lashes "put on hard" with a pair of chaps and the first day of the roundup to go on day herd.

The sentence was executed in good faith, except the day herding. Slim was too old and valuable a hand for work of this sort, and that part of the "court order" was never enforced.[7]

Often, in a session around the campfire or in the bunkhouse, cowboys would take turns at storytelling. The waddie without an amusing yarn to spin was a rarity, for it was the favorite pastime among range men. Generally the storytelling followed one of three patterns: the circular story, the tall tale, or the amusing anecdote.

The circular story was usually practiced by

---
[7] Albert W. Thompson, *They Were Open Range Days, Annals of a Western Frontier* (Denver, Colo.: World Press, Inc., 1946), pp. 32-35.

one of the older hands who had years of "chin-flappin' " experience, for it required a storyteller to hold his audience in suspense for as long as possible. The gist of the circular story is that the speaker begins with some particular place of action and talks in a "circle" until he eventually arrives back at the initial starting point and begins all over again. He will keep this up in all seriousness until the last listener has finally caught on. But sometimes the "goat" of the joke, if he were a stranger to the storyteller, would turn the tables by handing the joker a note stating that he was deaf and would appreciate the other telling his story over again, this time speaking louder.

Typical of tall tale telling is the one the cowboy spun about a gun he once owned which shot so hard it would have been against the law to fire it off in a civilized country. Once the gun went off accidentally and, in the interest of humanity, the cowboy followed the bullet. He had not gone far when he found a dead deer. Then, shortly, he came to where the lead had struck a tree limb, splitting it and catching the toes of a dozen turkey gobblers which had been roosting there. The bullet had then broken open a bee tree from which the cowboy had procured over a hundred pounds of wild honey. He admitted that, since you can't tell a bee tree by looking at it, this last was pure luck.[8]

This in turn might remind a fellow puncher of a gun he had once seen—the biggest buffalo gun ever to hit the plains. It was so big that it didn't have a caliber; and if it had been a shotgun, it wouldn't have had a gauge. While on the plains one day the cowboy had fired it at a buffalo bull. The bull fell as if dead but, when it was about half skinned, it came to life and took out after the waddie. The cowboy knew he couldn't run fast enough to escape, and there wasn't a place in sight where he could take cover. Then, just when it looked for certain that he was doomed, he suddenly realized that he had just one hope. Throwing down the buffalo gun, he ran up the barrel and let the bull go on past.[9]

The cowboy by no means invented the tall tale, but he proved that he had the capacity to dream up some good ones. Jack Thorp, respected and well-liked New Mexico rancher, loved to recite the tall story of old man Yost and his herd of dry-land terrapins.

Old man Yost was eating in a fancy San Antonio restaurant one day when he discovered that the

[8] Sam P. Ridings, *The Chisholm Trail; A History of the World's Greatest Cattle Trail* (Guthrie, Okla.:   Co-operative Publishing Company [c. 1936]) , pp. 316-17.

[9] *Ibid.,* pp. 312-13.

soup he was having was turtle soup and that it cost six bits a dish in Texas. Up North, it would sell for about two dollars. The cowman, having just gone broke in the cattle business after some trouble with his partner, thought of all the dry-land terrapins running around loose on the Texas prairies, multiplied that by two dollars a head, and came up with the total of $359,664 and ambitions to be the first man ever to drive a turtle herd north.

He rode back to his ranch and started gathering his herd. He sent his punchers out with gunny sacks tied to their saddle horns, and it wasn't long before they had corraled exactly 14,-986 turtles. The old man was chomping at the bit to be off, so they hit the trail with the herd.

From experience gained in rounding up the herd, Yost knew that he would have to keep the turtles on high ground, for if they struck a sandy flat they would likely stampede, attempting to dig themselves in. The cowboys discovered right away the uselessness of trying to throw their ropes, for the turtles would only duck back into their shells and dodge the loops. The first day they made a quarter of a mile's progress. After some more quick mathematics the old man saw that in only 5,600 days he would have his herd to market.

But he also thought of the fortune he would make and pushed on.

The months passed and, when late fall came, the herd was so restless it could hardly be held on the bed ground. The cowboys tried laying the turtles on their backs at night, but they found that the critters kicked their legs so much that they were too tired to travel the next day. And, after one cold night, they had to leave behind several hundred head because of frostbitten feet. Finally the herd reached the Red River. Yost was not worrying about crossing, for they had crossed other rivers without a single loss. But he didn't know that his former partner had heard about the terrapin herd and was jealously scheming to stop it.

As the herd pushed into the river, Yost noticed someone in a boat rowing out to place an object on a log in the middle of the stream. He didn't think anything about the matter but, when his turtle herd reached the log, every last one of them suddenly dove to the bottom of the river. Old man Yost later figured that right then and there he lost somewhere around half a million dollars. And all because his old partner was mean enough to put a *diving mud turtle* in front of his dryland terrapin herd![10]

---

[10] N. Howard (Jack) Thorp, as told to Neil M. Clark, *Pardner*

Even the cowboy's ordinary speech was rich
with humor; he was, in fact, a master at amusing,
picturesque phraseology which employed similes
and metaphors drawn from range life. Ramon
F. Adams, an expert on the subject of Western
speech, claims that listening to a group of cowboys talk among themselves is better than any
vaudeville show. In his *Cowboy Lingo*, he illus-
trates the cowboy's ability to paint word pictures
with a paragraph from a letter by Charlie Russell:

> Pat Riley was killed while sleepin' off a drunk at
> Grass Range. Pat took a booze joint and, after smokin'
> the place up and runnin' everybody out till it looked
> like it was for rent, fell asleep. The booze boss gets a
> gun and comes back and catches Pat slumberin'. Pat
> never woke up, but quit snorin'.[11]

At times the cowboy was capable of some good
wit. A story is told of a cowboy who was invited
by an English duke to have a drink with him in
Dodge City. Naturally, the invitation was accepted. Thus the two men—one schooled in the age-
old traditions of England and the other a product
of the American plains—bent elbows together. In
paying for the drinks, the Englishman reached
into his pocket and came out with an English

---

of the Wind (Caldwell, Idaho: The Caxton Printers, Ltd., 1945),
pp. 221-26.

[11] Ramon F. Adams, *Cowboy Lingo* (Boston: Houghton Mifflin
Company, 1936), pp. 237-38.

coin. Reminded by it of his heritage, the duke held the coin before the cowboy.

"You see the likeness of His Majesty, the king, on this coin? He made my grandfather a lord."

The cowboy looked the coin over solemnly, then dug into the pockets of his breeches and came out with a copper penny.

"Uh-huh," he said. "An' see the likeness of thet red Injun on this here penny? He made an angel outa my grandpappy!"[12]

Cow-country humor was more than mere story-telling and horseplay; it was an ingrained reaction, an *esprit de corps,* a philosophy common to the "jes' plain bow-legged humans" of the range. Without a doubt, the cowboy excelled any other vocational group when it came to integrating a sense of humor into everyday affairs. For him, there was little too serious or too sacred to have its humorous side.

---

[12] Ridings, *op. cit.,* p. 591.

Chapter II

The Windy West

*"One thing I'll say fer the West is that
in this country there is more cows and
less butter, more rivers and less water,
and you can look farther and see less
than in any other place in the world!"[1]*

IN THE HUMOR of every phase of our American
frontier there has been tall tale telling about the
wonders of nature. Lusty frontiersmen were forever ready to brag that their part of the world
had the biggest trees, the highest mountains, the

---

[1] Complaint of a Southwestern rancher.

hottest summers, the coldest winters, or the strongest winds of any. Such famous "liars" as Mike Fink of the Mississippi river-boat breed, Davy Crockett of the early Southwest, and Jim Bridger of the mountain men glorified their respective locales with imaginative yarns that tested the credulity of listeners.

The American cowboy was not beyond a similar vanity for the Land of the Cow Critters, or above telling a few lies to defend it. To him, there was no place that could measure shoulder-high to the range country, and he was not the least bit bashful about saying so. If an outsider should comment on some scenic wonder in a place foreign to the cow country, the cowboy could be counted on to top it with a wonder of his own, actual or otherwise.

One Westerner who had listened to an Easterner expound upon the majesty of a foreign waterfall promptly denounced it as "a mere watering-pot" and claimed that he could put up one that would squirt it to a finish.[2] Mostly, though, the cowboy stuck to subjects common to the range. One such was the amazing suddenness with which the weather could change on the open prairie. For example, one cowboy claimed that he always

---

[2] Philip Ashton Rollins, *The Cowboy: His Characteristics, His Equipment, and His Part in the Development of the West* (Reprint ed.; New York: Charles Scribner's Sons, 1936) , pp. 89-90.

carried with him three necessary items of apparel: a linen duster, a rain slicker, and a buffalo overcoat. Many times he had been forced to wear them all within the period of an hour.[3]

A newcomer to the West, unaware of how the climate could change so abruptly, once made himself four harness tugs out of green buffalo hide. The first time he used them he was caught in a sudden rainstorm that filled his wagon so full of water that he was forced to get out and walk beside his team. But when he got to where he was going, he turned about to find that his wagon was nowhere in sight. The rawhide had stretched in the rain, and the wagon was a full mile behind on the tugs. The greenhorn started back to find his wagon, but just then the sun suddenly appeared and dried the rawhide, which contracted so quickly that the wagon ran right over its owner and killed him.[4]

"Last summer I 'uz ridin' along," said one cowboy, "thinkin' as how the weather must be hotter'n Satan in long handles, when I hears a low moanin' behind me and turns 'round to see a blizzard whizzin' in. Right away I knows I got no time for admirin' th' scenery, so I jabs steel

---

[3] Joseph Kinsey Howard, *Montana; High, Wide, and Handsome* (New Haven, Conn.: Yale University Press, 1943), p. 148.

[4] *Ibid.* A similar yarn was spilled by Sam P. Ridings in *The Chisholm Trail*, pp. 316-17.

an' heads for home. That ol' hoss musta known about blizzards, too, 'cause 'fore I had time t' chaw my terbaccer twice, we 'uz there. But when I went to unsaddle the animal, danged if I didn't find its forequarters plum' foamy with sweat and its hindquarters frozen solid with ice where th' teeth of th' blizzard had caught it!"[5]

Another cowboy on a very hot day decided to go for a swim. When he had shucked his clothes, he walked to the edge of a cliff overlooking a stream and dove in. Just as he jumped, a drought dried up the stream. But he was in luck, for a sudden flash flood roared down the dry creek bed. The cowboy landed safely in the water but, by the time he came up for air, a Norther had swept in and frozen the surface into solid ice. He surely would have drowned had not the sun made a quick appearance and evaporated the stream dry again. As it was, all the cowboy got out of it was a bad sunburn before he could get his clothes back on again.[6]

Just about any cowboy who had endured a winter in a line shack was likely to have his version of how cold it could get. One told of the experience he had when the temperature

---

[5] J. Frank Dobie, *The Flavor of Texas* (Dallas, Tex.: Dealey & Lowe, 1936), pp. 17-20. An adaptation.

[6] Told by J. Frank Dobie, as quoted by Paul Bolton in "Texas Tall Tales," *Life*, November 1, 1943.

dropped so low that the flame of his candle froze stiff, and he had to wait until the flame thawed before he could put it out. Then, when the sun appeared, it became so hot that the corn he had for the stock began to pop. IIis horse thought the popcorn was snow and almost froze to death.

A couple of punchers were sent out to plant fence poles one winter day, and they found the ground littered with frozen rattlesnakes. Deciding to save the ranch some money, the waddies drove the snakes into the ground for fence poles. They rode back to the ranch feeling proud of themselves, but the next day they were fired by the foreman. The snakes had thawed out and crawled off with several miles of good barbed wire.[7]

"Cold!" exclaimed a puncher. "Why, it got so dern cold at our ranch one winter that the thermometer dropped to ninety-five degrees below zero. Our foreman came out to give us orders fer th' day, but the words froze as they came outa his mouth. We had to break 'em off one by one so's we could tell what he was sayin'."

Charlie Russell liked to tell of the time when a friend left a poker game in Great Falls, Montana, one winter night and froze to death on a

---

[7] Told by J. Frank Dobie, as quoted in "Life Goes to a Tall Tales Session in Texas," *Life*, June 1, 1942.

street corner. A listener would view that serious, weather-toughened face of Charlie's and comment how unfortunate that was.

"Oh, that wasn't so bad," Charlie would answer. "We hung a lantern on his ear and used 'im for a lamppost all winter."[8]

Another Montana range yarn is of the traveling salesman who was caught in an autumn blizzard and forced to spend the night at a hotel which offered only the scantiest of bedcovers. Even after piling everything he could find on his bed, he still shivered in agony. Finally he heard sounds of life below and stumbled downstairs. There in the lobby was a stage driver who had been facing the storm for hours, but who was now stripped to his long handles in an attempt to thaw out by the stove. The driver's breath had frozen to his mustache whiskers, and icicles hung down from his chin. The salesman looked at him in amazement and exclaimed: "My gosh! What room did *you* have?"[9]

It was generally the wind which caused the most comment from any new arrival on the Southwestern plains. But the stranger who asked, "Does the wind blow this way all the time?" was likely to gain the answer, "Heck, no. It blows the other

---

[8] Howard, *op. cit.*, pp. 148-49.
[9] *Ibid.*, p. 145.

direction about half the time." And when pushed for enlightenment on the subject, a cowboy would patiently explain that the best way to tell about the wind in those parts was to watch the heavy log chain hanging in front of the bunkhouse. If the chain was hanging at a forty-five-degree angle, there was probably a slight breeze blowing. But if the chain stood straight out, the chances were good that a real blow was up.

A waddie told of the time during a little gale when he tied his horse to a brush clump atop a sand dune and left. When he came back later, he looked around for his horse and could not find him. He had about decided that the animal had broken loose and drifted when he suddenly heard a whinny from above him. He looked up to find that his horse was dangling from the very top of a tall tree which he had mistaken for a bush before the wind had blown all the sand from around it.[10]

In one section of Texas it was so windy that a rancher had to put hinges on his house so that, when a big blow came along, the house would flatten out on the ground and afterwards could be pushed right up again. This was the same place that people had to feed their chickens buck-

---

[10] Mody C. Boatright, *Tall Tales from Texas;* foreword by J. Frank Dobie (Dallas, Tex.: Southwest Press, 1934), pp. 41-43.

shot to keep them from blowing away; but, any-how, the wind kept all the feathers blown off the fowls. One citizen claimed he witnessed a hen setting against the wind lay the same egg five times!

A rancher complained because the wind kept all the barbs of his barbed-wire fence blown to the corners, and another that a gale had taken away his cookstove and returned the next day for the lids and poker. This happened on the same day that the wind was so strong from the west that the sun was three hours late going down.

If the West wasn't the windiest place, it was the driest. When a cowboy heard a stranger comment that a certain river was once so dry that he crossed it without getting the tops of his shoes wet, the cowboy sniffed and commented:

"Heck, that ain't nuthin'! Why I onc't rode a steamboat down the Brazos when we couldn't see the banks fer the clouds of dust raised by th' paddle wheel!"

A wealthy Easterner once came West to try his luck at farming. The first year the pilgrim plowed and planted, but there was no rain. All his crops failed. The next year the same thing happened, and the next. By this time the fellow was getting pretty fed up with a country where no rain ever fell. But he was a stubborn gent. He decided that he was going to grow a crop if it took every cent he owned. He went to town and bought a wagon and put tall sideboards on it. Then he sent to some place outside the West and bought a bunch of good dirt. He put the dirt in the wagon, hitched the wagon to a pair of the fastest horses he could find, and then he hired a cowboy to drive the wagon.

"Now, keep your eyes open," he told the waddie. "I've got a crop planted in that wagon. If you see a cloud, I want you to drive like all get out until you are underneath it. Sooner or later it's going to let some moisture fall and, when it does, I want you to be there to catch every last drop."

He didn't know that the cowboy had lived in that part of the country all his life and had never once seen it rain. One day, sure enough, a cloud happened by and the cowboy took off after it. The Easterner watched from atop his windmill and, about sunset, he saw that cloud was letting some rain fall. Satisfied, he went about his affairs, but it wasn't half an hour before the wagon came tearing back into the yard. The cowboy jumped out, dripping wet, and ran up to his employer.

"I quit!" he said. "I've lived in this country

all my life, but I ain't never seen anything like it."

"What's the matter?" the Easterner asked. "A little rain isn't going to hurt you."

"I don't know about that," the cowboy answered. "But, Mister, you don't have enough money to hire me to go back. Why, I'll bet there was over five hundred wild geese flying along in that one lil' ol' cloud!"[11]

Another waddie who had never seen it rain was knocked unconscious when a couple of drops of water hit him on the forehead. His friends had to throw a bucketful of sand in his face before he came to.

About ten year ago (said Sacatone Bill) I got plumb sick of punchin' cows around my part of the country. She hadn't rained since Noah, and I'd forgot what water outside a pail or a trough looked like. So I scouted around inside of me to see what part of the world I'd jump to, and as I seemed to know as little of Colorado and minin' as anything else, I made up the pint of bean soup I call my brains to go there. So I catches me a buyer at Benson and turns over my pore little bunch of cattle and prepared to fly. The last day I hauled about twenty buckets of water and threw her up against the cabin. My buyer was settin' his hoss waitin' for me to get ready. He didn't say nothin' until we'd got down about ten mile or so.

"Mr. Hicks," says he, hesitatin' like, "I find it a good

---

[11] Based on a yarn told by Dale L. Morgan in *The Humboldt; Highroad of the West* (New York: Farrar & Rinehart, 1943), pp. 321-22.

A little rain never hurt anybody

rule in this country to overlook other folks' plays, but I'd take it mighty kind if you'd explain those actions of yours with the pails of water."

"Mr. Jones," says I, "it's very simple. I built that shack five years ago, and it's never rained since. I just wanted to settle in my mind whether or not that damn roof leaked."[12]

The story is told that during a great South-western drought, the preacher in one community sent out word that they all should meet at the church and pray for rain. One grizzled old-timer decided that it wouldn't hurt to try anything, so he attended the meeting. However, after the preacher had had his say concerning the benevolence of the Lord and made ready to begin the prayer, the old rancher stood up and shook his head.

"Hold up a minute," he said. "It ain't goin' to do any good prayin' fer rain when the wind is in the West!"[13]

The great vastness of the West and the enormous distances between points on the plains were often subjects for cowboy comment. One yarn tells of a Texan who saw one of his closest neigh-

[12] Stewart Edward White, *Arizona Nights* (New York: The Mc-Clure Company, 1907 [As reprinted by Hillman Periodicals, Inc., N.Y.]) , pp. 96-97.

[13] Mody C. Boatright, *Folk Laughter on the American Frontier* (New York: The Macmillan Company, 1949) , p. 135.

bors with all his goods piled on a wagon, evidently ready to leave the country. Since the man lived only some fifty miles away, the Texan was greatly concerned.

"You're not leaving for good?" he asked.

"Dern right!" answered the other. "This country is gettin' entirely too crowded for me. I found out the other day that some *hombre* has moved in down the river not over ten miles from my place. An' derned if he ain't been there a whole year. I'm headin' out for some place where a man either don't have any neighbors at all or at least knows the ones he's got."

Cowboys liked to tell about the Englishman who arrived in the West fresh from his crowded island home. On a bright morning the pilgrim looked across the plains to where the mountains, standing clear in the sunlight, appeared to be only a few miles away. Actually, it was nearly thirty miles to them; but the Englishman took out to hike to them, despite the warning from a couple of cowpunchers. That afternoon the punchers decided to ride out and see how he was progressing. When they caught up with him, about ten miles out, he was sitting beside a very small stream taking off his clothes. When they asked what he was doing, the Englishman announced that he was going to swim across the river. The cowboys told him that he was crazy to think of swimming a creek that was only a couple of feet wide and held only an inch of water.

"Hah!" said the Englishman. "I know I was fooled by those blarsted mountains, but I'll swim this river if it takes me all day!"[14]

Some of the new arrivals out West, though, found just a bit more elbowroom than they really preferred. On the door of a deserted nester's shack this sign was found:

>30 miles to water
>20 miles to wood
>10 inches to Hell
>Gone Back East to Wife's family[15]

Without a doubt the West was the healthiest place on earth. Especially Texas. Supposedly the Texas prairies were so healthy that few inhabitants ever died *naturally* there. Either they had the assistance of a bullet or else they grew so old that they just dried up and blew away. There is a story to the effect that some immigrants once

---

[14] N. Howard (Jack) Thorp, as told to Neil M. Clark, *Pardner of the Wind* (Caldwell, Idaho: The Caxton Printers, Ltd., 1945), pp. 205-6.

[15] Dobie, *The Flavor of Texas*, pp. 15-16.

met a very old man at the Texas border and, upon questioning him, found that he was so bored with the monotony of the ages that he was leaving Texas in hopes of finding some place where he could die like other people.

A young doctor came to the West hoping to build a good practice for himself. But he found that he could not sell his medicine to folks who had absolutely no use for it. The doctor finally had to turn to sharpening bowie knives for a living.

In some parts of the West it was all but impossible to raise watermelons because the soil was so rich and the vines grew so fast that the little melons were dragged over the ground and worn out before they could ripen.[16]

And, in another section, cows grew so old that wrinkles on their horns went to the very tip, making it necessary to attach corncobs to the horns for wrinkles to grow out on.

And, in another area, the prairie grasses grew so thick and fast that gophers often got choked to death coming out of their holes.

The folks of one neighborhood were forced to put bells on their children to save them from the enormous chicken hawks. But when a waddie

[16] Edward Everett Dale, *Cow Country* (Norman, Okla.: University of Oklahoma Press, 1945), p. 138.

told of a hawk with a wingspread of fifty feet
which he had shot down, a cowboy from another
section commented:

"Gosh! It musta been a young 'un."[17]

A cowboy who had a reputation for telling tall
ones was asked to make an offering one night,
but he refused. His grounds for not doing so
were that he had been telling one lie about an
elk with fifteen-foot horns for so long that he
had come to know the exact place he had shot
it. It seemed that it was so real, in fact, that one
night he climbed up in the loft to take a look
at the horns and doggoned if they weren't there![18]

But another "unexaggerating" cow poke told
of the time he had seen over two hundred thousand head of antelope on the prairie—all at once.
How many elk had he seen in a bunch? Well,
at least a million. And buffalo—not less than
three million. At that time his wagon train had
been kept busy for five days and nights shooting
their way through a buffalo herd. But they had
no sooner reached high ground than they looked
back and discovered how lucky they had been.

---

[17] *Ibid.*, p. 139.

[18] Charles M. Russell, *Trails Plowed Under;* illustrated in color
and line by the author (Garden City, N.Y.: Doubleday, Doran &
Company, Inc., 1936), p. 191.

The herd they had been in was only the stragglers. The main herd was just coming up.[19]

A favorite tale concerning the fertility of the soil is the one of the Brazos Valley citizen who accidentally dropped a kernel of corn near his back door. The corn sprouted and began growing with amazing speed. The man's young boy decided to climb the stalk but, after he had gone a ways, he became frightened and started back down. But the corn was growing upward faster than the boy could climb downward. Higher and higher the stalk and the boy went, until the father could no longer see his son. He ran and got his axe and began chopping on the stalk. But, though the axe bit deep, by the time he swung again the previous cut was out of reach.

The father never heard from his son again, but he knew the boy was still alive for, every now and then, a corncob would fall to the ground. It was only a short time later that the father died and went to Heaven. There he asked St. Peter if he had seen his son up that way. Upon hearing the boy's description and the story of what had happened, St. Peter nodded. He said that a boy answering to that description had passed through not long before, but that he was going too fast to stop.[20]

---

[19] *Ibid.*, pp. 193-94.
[20] Dale, *op. cit.*, pp. 138-39.

Chapter III

Cow Country Critters

*"Yuh gotta treat people jes' like yuh
do mules. Don't try to drive 'em. Jes'
leave the gate open a mite an' let 'em
bust in!"*[1]

WHENEVER COWBOYS weren't stretching their imaginations about the weather, they were generally dreaming up some wild yarns about the animals of the range country. Because cowboys lived close to nature, they understood and respected animal

---

[1] Edward Everett Dale, *Cow Country* (Norman, Okla.: University of Oklahoma Press, 1945), p. 143. An adaptation.

life. A range-wise man could foretell a bad winter by the coyote's extra-heavy fur or from noticing the beaver stocking up on saplings. Animals often offered the only companionship for long periods in the cowboy's life and, through intimate contact, he came to see their "human side" and to understand himself better as a "human animal."

Once a cow hand who had attended a fancy dinner party described himself as feeling like "an old ranch rooster flappin' his wings and tryin' to fly south in the winter."

Such application of human traits to animal life offered much possibility to the cowboys of the range and resulted in some of their most hilarious "windies." The intelligence of animals, for which the cowboy had a high regard, was generally the ignition subject for a barrage of high-soaring cowboy oratory which might include anything from hydrophobic skunks to rooter-dogs, a cross between a bulldog and a wild Mexican hog which was used to root out tarantulas and harvest goober peas. One story would lead to another until, at last, someone had produced the topper of them all.

A group of cowboys was sitting around arguing one lazy afternoon when one puncher began to brag about his dog, claiming that it was undoubtedly the smartest dog he had ever seen. He said that the dog had once been caught in a wolf trap by the tail.

"What yuh reckon that dog did?" he asked.

"Pulled up the stake and dragged it an' the trap back to the ranch," a waddie suggested.

The owner of the dog shook his head.

"Jes' turned around and bit his tail off," another tried.

"Naw, he didn't do none of them fool things."

"What did he do, then?"

"Why, he done jes' what any other sensible dog would've done. He jes' set up a howl and kept it up until I heard him and took the trap offen his tail!"[2]

A cowboy who had been listening to the conversation shook his head.

"Wal, now," he said. "I reckon I've never owned such a smart dog, but I did own an ol' hoss one time that was about the *dumbest* critter I ever did see. I'll tell yuh what that fool horse did one night when I drunk too much likker and passed out in town. He picked me up and slung me on his back and carried me twenty miles to the ranch. When he got me there, he pulled off my boots with his teeth and nosed me inta my bunk. Then he went to the kitchen,

---

[2] J. B. Polley, "Dock Burris Was Well Known," in *The Trail Drivers of Texas,* comp. and ed. by J. Marvin Hunter (2 vols. in 1; Nashville, Tenn.: Cokesbury Press, 1925) , p. 1017.

fixed up a pot of coffee, and brung me a cup all fixed up with cream and sugar. Then the next day I had a hangover, and he went out all by hisself and dug post holes all day so's the boss would let me sleep. When I woke up and found out what that fool hoss had done, I cussed him fer two days without stoppin' and wished 'im off on a greener which was passin' by. It was good riddance, too!"

"I'd say that was a pretty smart horse," observed a listener. "What in the world did you get rid of him for?"

"Smart, heck! Who ever heard of a real cowboy usin' cream and sugar in his coffee? No wonder I had such a turrible hangover!"

"Thet reminds me," piped up another waddie, "of a hoss a friend of mine down in Texas once owned. This here friend was plum' foolish over quail huntin', but he didn't have any bird dog. But he got to thinkin' that, since a cayuse is supposed to be the smartest animal alive, it ought to be able to do anything that a bird dog could do, so he taught it to point birds. It worked out pretty well, and he used that ol' hoss all one winter to hunt quail. But, come spring, this friend needed some breakin' out clothes, and he sold the hoss to a neighbor. But when the man took the hoss, my friend plum' fergot to tell him about its unusual ability. The next day the man came back with the animal and demanded his money back.

" 'Whut's wrong?' my friend asks.

" 'Wrong?' sez the new owner who is plainly disgusted. 'Heck, I can't even get the fool animal in the barn. Ever' time I try, he stops dead still with one foot lifted an' sticks his tail straight up in the air.'

"My friend thinks this over for a minute, then asks, 'You don't by any chance have some chickens around yore place, do you?'

" 'Why, yes,' sez the other, 'as a matter of fact, I got a chicken pen right next to the barn. Why?'

" 'Wal,' sez my friend, 'You don't have a thing to worry about, then. The next time that ol' hoss balks at the door, all you gotta do is shoot off yore gun and holler, "Missed again!" and he'll go right on in.' "

After this had been digested by all concerned, another waddie cleared his throat.

"That brings to mind," he said, "ol' Peg-Leg Dooley, who onc't had a rattlesnake for a pet. Now, you gents may figger I'm tryin' to string up a bunch o' nonsense, but I'll explain 'zactly how it happened. An', by the way, how ol' Pete got that peg leg.

"It seems ol' Pete was up in Oklahoma Terri-

tory one fall an' had to make camp in that shinnery country. Wal, he had heard how that country was full o' rattlesnakes, so he figgered he'd
tie a hammock up between two shinnery trees
when he bedded down. It was pretty dark by that
time, an' it was only after considerable gropin'
'round that Pete got his hammock tied up. Durin'
the night he felt that hammock swingin' quite
a bit, but he blamed it on the Oklahoma wind.
But the next morning when he woke up, derned
if he didn't find that he had tied that hammock
up with a pair of live rattlers!

"Wal, ol' Pete was pretty skitterish after that
an' packed up as quick as he could an' started
to kite outa there. But about that time his hoss
stepped in a gopher hole an' pinned him to the
ground. Pete was in a turrible fix an' thought
he was doomed to die right there, but he got
an idea that saved his life. He walked to the
nearest ranch an' borrowed an axe. Then he
came back and chopped off his leg and set hisself free.

"Then, after Pete had cut him a peg leg outa
a shin-oak tree, he skedaddled for home. When
he got there, he found a baby rattlesnake which
had struck him on the peg leg an' hadn't been
able to get loose. It was a cute lil' critter, an'
Pete decided to keep him for sort of a combi-

nation pet an' souveynir of his visit to Oklahomy.

"After that, Pete became real attached to that rattlesnake, which he named Elmer, an' Elmer to him. In fact, Elmer got so he was a regular watchdog an' guarded Pete's shack. One night, while Pete was gone, a thief busted into the shack, an' Elmer was on the job. He captured that ol' robber by wrappin' hisself around one o' the feller's legs an' a leg o' the table. Then he stuck his tail through the keyhole o' the door an' rattled until the law came.

"By and by Elmer grew up into one o' the biggest rattlesnakes anybody had ever seen. He wasn't so long, but he was about a foot thick. It got so he was the talk o' the whole country, an' ol' P. T. Barnum came down an' offered to buy him off Pete. But Pete was plum' sentimental about that snake, like I said, an' wouldn't let him go. But he got to thinkin' that he couldn't stand in the way o' fame an' fortune fer Elmer, an' agreed to loan him out to the circus.

"They stuck Elmer in a box an' hied him off in the baggage car of a train. Well, after a while Elmer got lonesome an' chewed his way outa the box. About that time the train started up a steep grade an' the couplin' busted. So what do you think ol' Elmer did? Why, he wrapped his head 'round one brake wheel and his tail 'round the other an' held the train together until they reached the next station! But all that strain on Elmer stretched him out until he was about thirty feet long. The circus had to advertize him as a boa constrictor instead of a rattlesnake!"[3]

It was time for one of the older hands to clear his throat and lope off on a yarn.

"Onc't, about twenty-thirty years ago when I wuz jes' a button, I wuz ridin' fer ol' Jim Creagor down on the border. Ol' Jim wuz as good a boss as a man ever hired on with, but sometimes he got the craziest ideas you ever heard of 'n wuz as stubborn as a longhorn bull about 'em. But all of us hard-ridin', fast-shootin' riders of the range managed to overlook most of ol' Jim's crazy notions 'n got along fine. That is, we did until the day he went down to Mexico City 'n came home with this fightin' game rooster.

"Right away it's clear that this ol' rooster 'n us cowboys ain't goin' to get along. He seems to figger right off that he's the king of the camp 'n struts 'round like he owned the place. Not that we cow pokes wuz foolish 'nough to get jealous of a lil' ol' chicken, but it kinda got under our skin the way he stuck his nose up at us.

---

[3] Stewart Edward White, *Arizona Nights* (New York: The Mc-Clure Company, 1907 [As reprinted by Hillman Periodicals, Inc., N.Y.]) , pp. 165-66. An adaptation.

Worse 'n that, ever' time we'd get in his way, that rooster'd tie off into a real temper'mental fit 'n come at us with spurs flashin'.

"Course our legs wuz pertected by our boots, but it wuz kinda like havin' a town dog yappin' at your heels. It got so we wuz walkin' 'round with one eye peeled in fear this chicken'd stage one of his attacks. Wal, we finally had all of that we could take, so we held a meetin' of the crew 'n kangarooed that bird. The decision was to execute him fer gen'ral misbehavior.

"But the minute we took out after him, he saw we wuz up to no good fer him. After that, he wuz no easy bird to catch, 'n he sure gave us eighteen waddies a go fer our money. A big, red-headed waddie by the name of Charlie Graham almost had him trapped on the barn roof. Charlie made a wild grab 'n ended up on the corral floor with a busted leg. But finally we got that rooster trapped between the corral fence 'n the barn, 'n though he put up plenty of fight he was over-powered by the force of numbers. Let me tell you, we wuz a scratched 'n bleedin' 'n mad bunch of cowboys by the time we got that rooster under control.

"We tied a blindfold over his eyes an' stood him up against a haystack 'n lined up twelve of our best shots fer a firin' squad. But jes' then ol'

It was like having a town dog yappin'
at your heels.

Jim came ridin' up 'n stopped the whole show. He said we ought to be ashamed of ourselves fer pickin' on sech a poor, defenseless chicken, made us untie 'im, 'n swore he'd fire the firs' so-'n-so that molest'd that bird without just cause.

"Wal, as you can imagine, after that things got even worse. That got to be the most overbearin' fowl I ever seen in my life. He'd slip up between our horses' legs 'n crow 'n make them range-wild cayuses so skeerish that it wuzn't even safe fer a bunch of bronc-bustin' experts like us. An' sometimes he'd come to the bunkhouse winder at two or three o'clock in the morning, jes' when we wuz sleepin' the soundest, 'n start crowin'. But he wuz too smart to ever bother us when the boss was around. An' we knew it would mean our job if we molest'd that chicken without a good reason.

"Meanwhile ol' Charlie Graham had been laid up with that broken leg, 'n all he did wuz sit around all day 'n nurse his hatred for that loud-lunged fowl. Then, one day, he got an inspiration 'n promised the boys that when they came in from work that night there'd be no more Mr. Rooster at that ranch.

"The boys had a hard time keepin' their minds on their chores that day in their eagerness to get back 'n see what Charlie had up his sleeve. Some

bet Charlie wouldn't have the nerve to buck ol'
Jim's orders, but when we rode in that night the
firs' thing we saw wuz the carcass of that rooster
lyin' in the yard about thirty feet from its head.
Charlie had a long, serious look on his face which
warned us to keep our mouths shut about the
hull thing. It wuzn't until later, in the bunkhouse, that Charlie started to laffin' so hard he
doubled up on the floor 'n rolled around. Finally,
when he got over his hysterics, he told us what
had happened.

"After we had rode out, Charlie had gone to
the barn 'n soaked a batch of blackberries in
some rotgut whisky which he had cached away fer
emergencies. Then he tossed a couple of hand-
fuls out in the corral where that rooster jcs'
gobbled 'em up like they wuz a real delight. But
after he had eat about fifteen blackberries, that
ol' chicken began to wobble around on his legs
'n when he'd peck at a berry he'd miss it about
four inches.

"About that time the boss came outa the house
'n started away on his horse. But he never got
to where he was goin', fer jes' then that rooster
saw him, threw back his head 'n let out a mighty
crow you could hear the length of the Brazos.
An' before ol' Jim knew what wuz goin' on, that

rooster charged up 'n sank a spur into the shank of Jim's hoss.

"Wal, to hear ol' Charlie tell it, the boss musta had time to recite the Lord's Prayer twenty times 'twixt the time he left that hoss's back 'n when he landed on his chin in the yard. An' when Jim set up 'n saw his prize game cock chasin' his hoss around the yard, he wuz madder'n twenty-nine hornets fightin' over a dead grasshopper. He got up and went into the house, 'n when he came out he had his .30-30 in his hands. It only took one shot to fix up Mr. Rooster.

"It wuz then that Charlie wandered up 'n inquired, innocent-like, as to why the boss had gone and shot that poor, defenseless chicken. Ol' Jim didn't have any answer at firs', 'n then he got that stubborn look on his face 'n said, 'He wuz guilty of disturbing the peace!' An' that wuz the last word he ever said about his prize game cock."

It was then that the stranger stepped up and licked his lips solemn-like.

"Speakin' of chickens," he said, "calls to mind the time I decided to give up cowboyin' and go into the chicken business. And all because one day I got to thinkin' about how I could make a million dollars by mixin' up the breedin' a mite so's to get a chicken with a lot of thigh and breast and not much neck. I took one kind of chicken that was a squat little critter with a short neck and a big breast and crossed it with another kind that was built somethin' like a road runner, with big feet and long legs which made it stand about three feet tall. But somehow the product of my efforts wasn't at all like I expected.

"When the firs' bunch hatched, it turned out they was the strangest lookin' critters you ever saw. Their legs was so long and their necks so short that they couldn't reach the ground to feed themselves. I had to fix up a special table for 'em so's they wouldn't starve to death. And then next I found out that their feet was so big that ever' time the wind blew one over, it couldn't get back up by itself. It got so's I spent all my time runnin' around settin' 'em back right-side up.

"I was about to give the whole thing up but, luckily for me, that was the year of the great grasshopper plague. My chickens could catch about any kind of a bug that made the mistake of gettin' in the air, 'cause with them long legs they was the fastest things in the country. I used to set on my back porch and watch them chicks by the hour as they galloped to and fro around the hills catching grasshoppers, and I began to feel real proud and sentimental towards 'em.

"But the day came when I knew I had to start reapin' a return on my experiment, so I decided to take a bunch of the critters to market. I found, howsomever, that they was too tall to fit into a chicken crate like they was supposed to, and I had to turn the crate up sideways to get 'em in it. When I got to town I ran smack into a tourist party who was plum' astounded when I told that what I got in my crate is chickens. One lady decided to buy one of 'em as a souveynir of her trip out to the woolly West.

"It was about a month later that I got a letter from this Eastern lady tellin' me how that bird had died out of homesickness for the wide open spaces where it could run and romp in freedom. After that, I decided against sellin' any more of the birds unless the buyer promised to kill it and eat it quick, without makin' it suffer. But this lady also sent back the carcass of the bird which she had tried to eat, and requested that I get her teeth loose from it and send 'em back.

"Meanwhile, my other birds was gettin' friskier by the day, and I was havin' trouble keepin' 'em in their pens since they was gettin' so's they could run and jump clean over a ten-foot fence. They got so rambunctious, in fact, that I was wearin' myself out when I went to call 'em in for chuck. Finally, one day I got the idea of fixin' up a horn and trainin' those chickens to come runnin' at the honk-honk of that horn.

"You'd be surprised how quick my chickens was to learn about that honk-honk. I was real proud of 'em, and I named 'em the Honk-honk breed. We was gettin' along jes' fine until one day one of them automobeels came jarrin' down the road and, jes' as it passed my chicken ranch, it let out a honk-honk. Wal, you talk about a stampede! In a flash ever' last head of my Honk-honks sailed over my fence and took out after that car and outran it and scared the livin' daylights out of the driver.

"It got so's ever' time a car would come whizzin' by, my Honk-honks would be waitin' for it and then outrun it jes' to show off. I saw my chance to make that fortune I was after, and I started puttin' my birds up against any man, horse, or machine in those parts and bettin' on 'em. It was then that my faith in my Honk-honk birds began to pay off in cash."

Someone coughed and finally asked the question.

"If you wuz makin' so much money, how come you ain't in the chicken bizness today?"

"Wal, it's like this," the stranger explained. "Them Honk-honk hens jes' wasn't used to all that success and glory. It was race suicide, that's what it was. They got so gawd-awful big-headed

and haughty that they was too proud to stoop
so low as to lay an egg."[4]

In Dodge City, one of the woolliest of trail
towns, a tinhorn made the mistake of arguing
over cards with Dodge's marshal, Mysterious
Dave Mather. Dave was no slow man with a six
gun, having put six on the deceased list, all in
one night and in one sitting. The gambler drew,
and Dave drew faster. He not only hit his man,
but the bullet continued on through his victim
killing a hound dog that happened to be around
the saloon.

Now, the incident would have been closed and
forgotten if it had been merely a matter of burying one dead tinhorn gambler. But, as it was,
the hound dog happened to belong to a man
named Jim Kelly. Kelly owned only something
less than a hundred dogs which he kept to chase
jack rabbits, antelope, and coyotes. To some he
was known as "Dog Kelly," but not to his face.
Kelly was an Irishman with a Irish-sized temper
and, when he heard that Dave had killed one
of his dogs, he promptly went looking for him
with a sawed-off shotgun.

Dave, however, had been hit on the top of
his head by some plaster which had been knocked

---

[4] *Ibid.*, pp. 166-76.

loose by the gambler's shot, and he had gone to get his head wound fixed. When Kelly stormed into the saloon, the boys tried to cool him off about the dog and convince him that it was just an accident. But Kelly claimed that Dave, marshal or not, had no business shooting his gun off in the saloon without first looking to see if any of Kelly's dogs were around. They finally pacified Kelly by promising to bury the dog with military honors and to hold an inquest for the dead critter.

Someone sent for O. B. "Joyful" Brown, the coroner, to hold the inquest. A jury was impaneled, and several witnesses testified that they had never seen the dog take a drink and therefore it was doubtful if it had any business in the saloon anyhow. Other witnesses testified that Dave's gun had hung fire, and that if the dog had been on guard it could have jumped out of the window. Anyhow, the dog should have been out chasing jack rabbits, or at least kept one eye on Dave's gun which had a habit of going off unexpectedly.

The jury brought in the verdict that the dog they were then sitting on came to its death by a bullet fired from a gun in the hands of Dave Mather, better known as "Mysterious Dave," and that the shooting was done in self-defense and was perfectly justified as any dog should know better than to go to sleep in a Dodge City saloon.

This cooled Dog Kelly off somewhat but, to further pacify the Irishman, a hearse was hired and the famous Dodge City Cowboy Band led a regular funeral procession to Boot Hill where the dog was buried. A sermon was said over it, and then the boys all joined together in singing "The Cowboy's Lament." When it was over, Kelly went home with tears flowing down his cheeks, and Mysterious Dave, the gun-slinging marshal of Dodge City, breathed a sigh of relief and ordered the undertaker to clean up the carcass of the gambler from the saloon floor. The tinhorn was buried quietly and without ceremony.[5]

------

[5] John James Callison, *Bill Jones of Paradise Valley, Oklahoma; His Life and Adventures for Over Forty Years in the Great Southwest* (Chicago, Printed by M. A. Donohue, 1914), pp. 153-58.

Chapter IV

Law Without Order

"Shoot 'em up Joe.
Run for sheriff 1872.
Run from sheriff 1876.
Buried 1876."[1]

To THE COW COUNTRY, "law and order" was a
rather loose term. It could mean anything from
a decision by the Chief Justice of the Supreme
Court to the personal opinions of some grim-
mouthed gentlemen who were calmly tossing a
lariat over the limb of a cottonwood tree. Most

---

[1] From a tombstone in Boot Hill, Dodge City, Kansas.

Westerners liked the law well enough but weren't sure that it ought to be out West, and the respect that many had for it varied proportionately with the quickness of the sheriff's gun hand. All in all, the range felt that it had a pretty good set of rules of its own and resented outside interference. In fact, in some sections the name "son-of-a-gun stew" was changed to "district attorney stew."

This indifference to formal law was reflected in the courts of law of the West. On one occasion two attorneys had heatedly continued their argument after the jury had withdrawn. When accused of misreading a point of law, one attorney lost his temper and called the other a dirty, lying dog. His opposition countered with a like estimation. The courtroom quieted in anticipation of hearing the judge assess fines upon the lawyers. However, he spoke calmly.

"I'm happy that you two gentlemen are acquainted with one another. May we proceed with the case now?"[2]

In another court a certain lawyer who was noted for his oratorical abilities undertook to discuss at great length a point not entirely relevant to the case. As he was about to reach the emo-

---

[2] Based on a story in Mody C. Boatright, *Folk Laughter on the American Frontier* (New York: The Macmillan Company, 1949), p. 118.

tional peak of his delivery, a jackass suddenly began singing outside the courthouse window. The attorney for the opposition came to his feet.

"If the court pleases," he announced gravely, "I would like to second the opinion of the attorney on the outside."

During early Fort Smith, Arkansas, days a horse thief was brought before Judge Isaac C. Parker. The man was given a severe tongue-lashing and fined two hundred dollars. Upon hearing the fine, the horse thief thought he was going to get off lightly and jerked a big roll of bills from his pocket. He began to peel off twenties.

"And twenty years in prison," Parker added. "See if you can pull that out of your pocket."[3]

Another young citizen of the West was arrested for horse thievery and brought to trial. The evidence was overwhelmingly against him, but his lawyer went around the facts of the case, concentrating on the more emotional values in the accused's widowed mother, wife, and children. As a final touch he called upon the jury to gaze into the face of the defendant to see if they could find the look of a guilty man. They evidently

---

[3] Jack Martin, *Border Boss; Captain John R. Hughes, Texas Ranger* (San Antonio, Tex.: The Naylor Company, 1942), p. 12. A similar yarn is told in 89ers Association, Oklahoma City, *Oklahoma, the Beautful Land* (Oklahoma City, Okla.: The Times-Journal Publishing Company, 1944), p. 99.

did not, for they retired and came back with a quick "not guilty" verdict.

After the trial, a friend of the young man came up to him and asked confidentially, "Did you really steal that hoss or not?"

"Wal," the cowboy said, scratching his head, "I really can't say. I thought I did but, after hearin' that there lawyer's speech, derned if I'm so sure!"[4]

Most infamous of all Western courts was that of Judge Roy Bean, of Langtry, Texas. Roy was known to be much less interested in justice than in the jingling in the pockets of whoever might be so unfortunate as to stand accused before him. One of his most recounted decisions concerned the occasion when the body of a dead man was found near Langtry. On the corpse was a six-shooter and forty dollars, but no identification. Judge Bean stuck the six-shooter in his belt and the forty dollars in his pocket. When someone asked by what authority he thought he could take the money, he replied that he had tried the man and fined him for carrying a concealed weapon.[5]

---

[4] Based on a story by Mody C. Boatright, *op. cit.*, pp. 125-26.

[5] Based on a story told by C. L. Sonnichsen in *Roy Bean; Law West of the Pecos* (New York: The Macmillan Company, 1943), p. 127.

Sometimes, out West, it didn't do a bit of good to be dead!

This opinion was reversed, however, when a friend of Bean's was brought to court on charges of carrying a concealed weapon. He said that if his friend had been standing still when arrested, then he obviously was not *carrying* a weapon. And if he was moving, then he was *traveling*, and travelers had a legal right to carry weapons.[6]

One trial in Judge Bean's court involved a young, eager lawyer who continually objected to Bean's rulings and judicial opinions. Bean overruled him in every case. But when the lawyer threatened to *habeas corpus* his client, the judge angrily threatened to hang the lawyer if the man did not use more respectful language in the courtroom. The case was dropped for lack of a prosecuting attorney.[7]

A notable murder trial was under way in an Oklahoma territorial court and one of the lawyers, a heavy drinker, went to sleep during a noon recess. When the trial got under way again, the lawyer continued to sleep and could not be awakened. The judge cast a glance at the man, then asked, "Gentlemen of the bar, what shall we do with him?"

---

[6] *Ibid.*, pp. 90-91.
[7] *Ibid.*, pp. 86-87.

The opposing counsel rose. "I move the Court order him poured back into the bottle."

"So ordered."[8]

Cattle auctioneers are quite often known under the honorary title of "Colonel," and one was once called on to testify in court. The prosecuting attorney worked very hard to knock a dent in the colonel's testimony, but did not succeed. Angry at his failure, the lawyer took up the weapon of sarcasm.

"You call yourself a colonel," he said. "Now, just what were you a colonel in?"

"Wal," the other returned without hesitation. "I reckon you'd call it the cow brigade."

The lawyer gave one of his most potent sneers. "Then you're really not a colonel at all?"

"No," the auctioneer replied calmly. "It's just just like the 'Honorable' in front of your name —it don't mean a thing."[9]

One of the best "sure thing" men that ever hit the town of Dodge City was Mr. Bobby Gill. Once, when he was broke, Bobby was arrested for some minor offense and brought before the

[8] 89ers Association, Oklahoma City, *Oklahoma, the Beautiful Land* (Oklahoma City, Okla.: The Times-Journal Publishing Company, 1944), p. 99.

[9] Paul I. Wellman, *The Trampling Herd* (New York: Carrick & Evans, Inc., 1939), pp. 81-82.

police court. He was fined twenty dollars and costs. Now Bobby was no small-timer, and around Dodge City he had gained certain recognition. The marshal felt sorry for his having to face such a small fine and offered to throw off his part of the costs. The clerk agreed to do the same, and the judge said, "So will I. Now, Mr. Gill, do you have anything to say for yourself?"

Bobby rose promptly. "Your Honor," he said, "I have never yet been outdone in generosity, and I won't be now. I will throw off the fine."[10]

Big Mike, Irish of course, was being tried on a serious charge, yet he refused counsel, saying that he would defend himself. As the trial progressed, Mike, who knew nothing about legal procedure, made a continual bother of himself by interrupting testimonies and yelling at the prosecuting attorney. Finally the judge told Mike in plain language to sit down and shut up, adding:

"You'll get justice in this court."

"Begorra!" cried Mike. "That's what I'm afraid of!"

In *Tombstone,* Walter Noble Burns tells the story of S. C. Bagg, editor of the *Prospector,* who criticized in his paper a decision rendered by

---

[10] R. M. Wright, *Dodge City, the Cowboy Capital, and the Great Southwest in the Days of the Wild Indian, the Buffalo, the Cowboy, Dance Halls, Gambling Halls and Bad Men* (Wichita, Kan.: Wichita Eagle Press, c. 1913), p. 225.

Judge W. H. Barnes of the District Court and was fined five hundred dollars for contempt. Bagg had money enough but, as a matter of principle, he refused to pay the fine. Barnes ordered him committed to jail, where Bagg remained for several weeks, editing his paper from his cell and enjoying immensely his martyrdom. He even refused to accept the help of his friends, and finally the sheriff had to throw him out and lock the jail doors after him.

Several years later, Judge Barnes, then retired from the bench, was sent to jail for contempt by Judge R. E. Sloan. As he passed through the prison doors, he was on the verge of collapse and was sustained only by the sympathy of his friends. His spirits were lifted when a messenger arrived with a telegram.

"Friends from afar have heard of this damnable outrage," he declared and ripped open the envelope.

"Are you there Moriarty?" it read. It was signed by S. C. Bagg.[11]

One prisoner brought before Judge Parker was a slim-faced, balding man with beady eyes. He was charged with bigamy.

---

[11] Walter Noble Burns, *Tombstone, an Iliad of the Southwest* (Garden City, N.Y.: Doubleday, Page & Company, 1927), p. 35.

The judge was mostly interested in the jingle in the pockets of the accused.

"Your name?" asked the judge.

"Lee Galcatcher."

Parker looked over his glasses at the man, then turned to the bailiff.

"Take him back. This man couldn't be guilty of bigamy. He never caught a gal in his life."

On another occasion in Parker's court a witness for the prosecution was testifying as to the character of the complainant. The defense attorney was seeking to lay the predicate for impeaching the witness's testimony.

"You will admit, won't you," asked the attorney, "that the complainant has a good deal of trouble with his neighbors, that he quarrels often and has had several fights recently?"

"Yes," admitted the witness. "I know that."

"And you know, too, that he gets drunk and beats up his wife and that, last spring, he nearly whipped his young son to death? And you are aware that this man is arrested for being drunk nearly every time he comes to town, that he spends most of his time in jail?"

"Sure," agreed the character witness, "I know all those things."

"What!" cried the lawyer. "You admit knowing all about this man, and yet you swear that his reputation is good in your community?"

"Yes," returned the witness earnestly. "It takes more than that to get a bad reputation where I come from."

Irishman Justice Joyce presided over the Hays City, Kansas, court with an iron hand. One day an Irishman was brought to court for having killed a fellow railroad section hand with a shovel in an argument. There had been no one present to witness the affair, and it seemed the court would have to take the word of the prisoner as to what happened. When it came time to plead, the accused was asked:

"Guilty or not guilty?"

"Guilty, yer Honor."

Justice Joyce leaned over the bench and glowered at his fellow Irishman.

"Shut up," he rasped. "I discharge you for want of evidence."[12]

The courts thus reflected the attitude of the range country toward written law. Inevitably, a cowboy or a rancher would choose to settle his difficulties outside the courtroom according to the custom of cow country society. Most cowboys felt as did the old-timer who was telling a younger hand of the days when horse thieves were hanged first and tried afterwards.

---

[12] Wright, op. cit., p. 10.

"We never did hang the wrong one but once or twice," he said, "an' them fellers needed to be hung anyhow jes' on general principles."[13]

The rangeland had strict ideas on the matter of stealing, particularly of horses and cattle; yet it could not deny the fact that some of the largest and most respected brands to grow up in the West were ones of dubious beginnings. Cowboys liked to tell of the tenderfoot who arrived in the West with nothing more than one lone steer and a branding iron and ended up with a herd of fine cattle. Undeniably it was a capable steer, yet no more so than the cows of a rancher which invariably produced twins and frequently triplets, while the calfless cows of the other neighboring ranches persisted in hanging around this man's corral and bawling. The other ranchers finally had to threaten to hang the man if his cows continued to produce more than one calf at a time.[14]

One cowboy said, in speaking of another whose calves sometimes bore rather vague brands:

[13] Emerson Hough, *The Story of the Cowboy* (New York: Grosset & Dunlap, 1897), p. 107.

[14] Joseph Kinsey Howard, *Montana; High, Wide and Handsome* (New Haven, Conn.: Yale University Press, 1943), p. 108. Ernest Staples Osgood quotes Bill Nye on the same subject in *The Day of the Cattleman* (Minneapolis: University of Minnesota, 1929), p. 86.

"Ol' Bill is the most kindhearted soul yuh ever saw. He jes' can't stand to see a dogie wanderin' around without a mark on it. He's always givin' one a brand with his own iron."[15]

Cattlemen were not e n t i r e l y unreasonable about the matter. They could accept an occasional loss of a calf to a hungry nester or a wayfaring cowboy. One old cowman rode up one day to the chuck wagon of an outfit which was enjoying choice steaks from a freshly killed calf. The hide, wearing the cowman's brand, was hanging in plain sight. The foreman of the outfit invited the cattleman to light and join them. The rancher did, but could not resist the mild comment that "every outfit ought to eat its own beef." The foreman nodded in agreement.

"I reckon that's so," he said. "But fer some reason, your beef always seems to taste a little better than ours. Try some?"

And the rancher joined the grinning crew and helped them finish off the meat which he had unintentionally furnished.[16]

Another time, on joint roundup, a cowman spied a calf with another brand sucking one of his cows. Obviously, the calf had been misbrand-

---

[15] Ramon F. Adams, *Cowboy Lingo* (Boston: Houghton Mifflin Company, 1936) , p. 160.

[16] Wellman, *op. cit.,* p. 115.

ed; but, with cow country diplomacy, the rancher rode over to the foreman of the other brand and engaged him in conversation.

"I seen a funny thing 'while ago," he said at length. "One o' your calves 'uz followin' one o' my cows around an' bawlin' an' talkin' to her. It sez, 'Mama! Mama! Them old LFD boys jes' chased me around and roped me and dragged me an' slapped that big LFD on my shoulder, an' I wanted a nice little U like you have, Mama!'"

The rancher let this soak in, then went on. "I felt plumb sorry for the lil' critter, an' I reckon he's right. Another one o' them big LFD's would spoil th' poor thing's hide, an' I don't reckon any o' your boys would want to do that to him, would they?"[17]

Cowboys had a lot of fun with brands. They often spent their spare moments tracing patterns and figures for brands in the sand, figuring out new ones or ways to alter old ones. Some of the cowboys did it for fun—and some tried to make a business out of it. The story goes that a rancher whose brand was "IC" found that a rustler had been working it over to read "ICU." But the rancher went him one better. He held a round-

---

[17] J. Evetts Haley, *George W. Littlefield, Texan* (Norman, Okla.: University of Oklahoma Press, 1943) , pp. 151-52.

up and rebranded. This time his brand read: "ICU2."[18]

A similar yarn tells of a man who moved into a new country which was infested with thieves. His brand was B4. The thieves changed it to B4U, but the rancher got in the final word with the mark: B4U2.[19]

Horse stealing was a more serious matter, generally, than the rustling of cattle for the simple reason that horses were more vital to the livelihood in the West, especially for the cowboy. It was not entirely a matter of affection for him, for a cowboy afoot was a cowboy in a fix. Because of this, horse stealing was often an offense of serious consequence, whereas mere cow stealing could, in many cases, be taken tongue-in-cheek. Yet, even horse thievery was not beyond the range of cowboy humor.

For instance, there was the cowboy who rode into Tombstone on a eye-catching mount and put him up at a livery stable. A local citizen happened to see the horse and offered the stranger a good price for him. The man accepted the offer, and the transaction was made. When asked if the

---

[18] Oren Arnold and John P. Hale, *Hot Irons; Heraldry of the Range* (New York: The Macmillan Company, 1940), p. 107.

[19] Jules Verne Allen, *Cowboy Lore* (San Antonio, Tex.: The Naylor Printing Company, 1933), p. 29.

title on the horse was good, the cowboy looked up from counting his money and nodded.

"Wal, it is good enough jes' so long as you go west. But I wouldn't take that hoss east if I were you. The title ain't quite so good in that direction."[20]

In Texas a cowboy pleaded "not guilty" on a horse stealing count and, because his lawyer gave him able defense, he was adjudged to be innocent by the jury. The judge told the cowboy that he was a free man. The cowboy started to leave the courtroom, then turned back to the judge with a puzzled look.

"Jedge," he asked, "does this mean I can keep the hoss?"

And you just can't get much more innocent than the cowboy in the verses of "On the Dodge":

> Last week I found a stake-pin I had lost,
> Jest an iron one—'bout a dollar it had cost—
>   On it was tied a rope,
>   En it almost got my goat,
> When I found the other end tied to a horse!
>
> I'm as innocent as any man can be,
> But I'm afraid the Judge will not agree,

[20] Willam M. Breakenridge, *Helldorado, bringing the Law to the Mesquite* (Boston and New York: Houghton Mifflin Company, 1928) , p. 160.

As there isn't any use
In dishin' up a poor excuse,
I might as well jest saddle up and flee![21]

Another horse thief had been arrested, tried and, after much debate, was found to be innocent by a jury. The jury filed back into the courtroom and the foreman made his speech. It took him over an hour to tell in fancy oratory that the defendant had been found innocent of all charges. But the judge shook his head.

"You'll have to reconsider," he said. "The defendant was hung a couple of hours ago."

From New Mexico comes the story of a rancher who returned home to find several head of his fine horses missing. The rancher immediately saddled up and rode off. Several days later he returned to the ranch with all his horses, and he had nothing to say about their disappearance until someone finally asked what had happened to the thief.

"Wal, it's like this," he explained. "I followed the tracks for two days, an' late in the evening of the second I came onto this *hombre* drivin' my hosses. I caught him an' put him with his

---

[21] N. Howard (Jack) Thorp, as told to Neil M. Clark, *Pardner of the Wind* (Caldwell, Idaho: The Caxton Printers, Ltd., 1945), p. 134.

hands tied on one of the hosses an' headed back. Night came, and we had to make camp. In order to keep this feller from leavin', I left him on the hoss, tied a rope 'round his neck, and hitched the other end to a tree limb. I figgered this would keep him in place, so I went to sleep. But, yuh know, the next morning I woke up, an' there that *hombre* was danglin' from that limb. I had plum' fergot to stake that hoss to keep it from grazin' off during the night!"[22]

A cowboy with a shady reputation asked a cattleman for a riding job. The rancher was skeptical, but agreed to give the man a chance to show what he could do. That evening at the corral he told the cowboy to rope a certain horse. The waddie tried several loops and missed them all. He tried to use darkness as an excuse.

"Darkness, heck!" e x p l o d e d the disgusted rancher. "Your trouble is that all your ropin' experience has been at night instead of in the daytime!"

While visiting a sheep camp, two cowboys noticed some Navajo blankets and, on the grounds that sheepmen aren't human, decided to steal and sell them. Rather than take the blankets back to camp, the waddies cached them by burying them in the ground. It was agreed that they

---

[22] Arnold and Hale, *op. cit.*, p. 99.

would return together later, get the loot, and take it to town and sell it. But one cowboy got to thinking about the matter, and decided that it would be better to have all rather than half the amount for which they could sell the blankets. But when he returned to where they had hidden them, he found an empty hole in the ground and a note from his buddy: "I got to thinkin', Charlie, it ain't right to steal. You done wrong to take them blankets. So I'm takin' 'em all, so's you won't have no stolen goods, and your con-shense won't worry you none."[23]

The business of law enforcement also had its lighter moments. A cowboy who had killed a real-estate salesman in a gun duel reported the incident to the sheriff and offered to give himself up. He asked the law officer what he would get for committing such a crime.

"Shucks!" snorted the lawman. "You won't get nothin'. We took the bounty off them fellers a long time ago!"[24]

Sheriff Elfego Baca of New Mexico once sent

[23] Gladys Shaw Erskine, *Broncho Charlie; a Saga of the Saddle; the Life Story of Broncho Charlie Miller, the Last of the Pony Express Riders* (New York: Thomas Y. Crowell, 1934), pp. 190-92.

[24] Federal Writers' Project, *Idaho Lore*, edited by Vardis Fisher (Caldwell, Idaho: The Caxton Printers, Ltd., 1939), pp. 126-27.

a deputy out to get a certain bad *hombre* who had broken jail. The deputy was gone for nearly a week before Sheriff Baca received from him a very lengthy telegram which told in detail of the capture of the bad man and of the deputy's heroic efforts in achieving same. It ended by asking Baca, "What do I do with him now?"

The deputy received his answer in exactly ten words: "Kiss him twice and bring him in, you dern fool."[25]

Actually, the main distinction in the attitude of the range toward the matter of crime was whether the act had been committed against the range society or against some foreign element. Largely the cowboy's interpretation of the law was made in very much the same vein as when Judge Bean was trying a man who was believed guilty of killing a Chinese railroad worker.

"Gents," so goes the infamous ruling, "I've read this here book of statutes from cover to cover, an' I'll be hanged if I can find anywhere which says it's agin the laws of the State of Texas to kill a Chinaman. Therefore, I find the defendant 'not guilty'!"[26]

---

[25] Kyle S. Crichton, *Law and Order, Ltd.; the Rousing Life of Elfego Baca of New Mexico* (Santa Fe: New Mexico Publishing Corporation, 1928), pp. 105-7.

[26] Based on a story by C. L. Sonnichsen, *op. cit.,* p. 119.

Chapter V

The Quick and the Dead

Deer sur, we have brand 800 caves this roundup we have made sum hay potatoes is a fare crop. That feller yu lef in charge at the other camp got to fresh and we had to shoot him. Nothing much has hapened since yu lef. Yurs truely, Jim.[1]

THE WILD WEST settled her social problems in some very special ways which included six-shooter law, bullet battles, vigilante raids, and necktie

---

[1] Emerson Hough, *The Story of the Cowboy* (New York: Grosset & Dunlap, 1897), p. 35. An adaptation.

parties. None of these methods evidenced any great amount of tact or diplomacy, but they were pretty effective in clearing away misunderstandings. The Old West was a place of sudden violence, where the strong conquered; and to be strong generally meant to be quick and sure with a six gun. Accordingly, the men of the West developed great respect for swiftness of the gun hand.

They also possessed an extremely realistic attitude toward death. That final shuffling off of the coils was altogether too present in the cowboy's existence to grieve long about. It had to be accepted as philosophically as it was possible to do so, in the attitude that the inevitable merely came sooner than it might have.

A cowboy who had lost out in a six-shooter argument was being buried by his friends. After the sod had been heaved upon his box, someone "sorta felt a few words orter be said." A Church of England prayer book was produced by a rancher's wife, and someone read out the verse about the "quick and the dead." As he turned sadly from the grave, one puncher shook his head to another.

"Ol' Bill wasn't very quick," he observed, "but he sure is dead."[2]

---

[2] Albert W. Thompson, *They Were Open Range Days, Annals of*

This same acceptance of death is found in the lines penned by a sagebrush scribe:

When men lived raw in the desert's maw,
And Hell was nothing to shun.
Where they buried 'em neat
    without preacher or sheet,
And writ on their headboards
    crude but sweet,
"This jasper was slow with a gun."[3]

In her *Between Sun and Sod,* Willie Newbury Lewis tells of an old Dutchman rancher whose wife had died. The Dutchman was very sad and, wishing to pay tribute to the woman who had shared his life and troubles, commented in typically Western laconic style, "Doc, it would've been easier for me to give up my best span of mules than that old woman."[4]

On another occasion a local no-good was caught cheating in a poker game and was promptly shot to death by one of his fellow participants. The fellow was married, and it was agreed that someone should notify his wife. Of course no one wanted the chore, so the matter was decided by drawing cards. The loser was a gambler. Re-

a *Western Frontier* (Denver, Colo.: World Press, Inc., 1946), p. 179.

[3] *Ibid.,* p. 193.

[4] Willie Newbury Lewis, *Between Sun and Sod* (Clarendon, Tex.: Clarendon Press, 1938), p. 179.

luctantly, with hat in hand, he knocked on the
door of the victim's shack, and a big, straggly-
haired female answered the door. The gambler
asked to see Widow Yates.

"Widder Yates? My name is Yates, but I ain't
no widder."

"Lady," the gambler said, "I have twenty dollars that says you are!"[5]

In Virginia City an outlaw named Boone Helm
was about to be hanged. Beside him writhed a
member of his outlaw gang.

"Kick away, old fellow," said Boone. "I'll be
in Hades with you in a jiffy. Every man for his
principles. Hurrah for Jeff Davis. Let 'er go,
men!"[6]

And Black Jack Ketchum had this comment
to make as he was about to be hanged at Clayton,
New Mexico:

"Can't you hurry this up a bit? I hear they
eat dinner in Hades at twelve sharp. I don't aim
to be late."[7]

---

[5] Based on a story by Mody C. Boatright in *Folk Laughter on
the American Frontier* (New York: The Macmillan Company,
1949), pp. 18-19.

[6] Philip Ashton Rollins, *The Cowboy, His Characteristics, His
Equipment, and His Part in the Development of the West* (Reprint ed.; New York: Charles Scribner's Sons, 1936), p. 159.

[7] George D. Hendricks, *The Bad Man of the West* (San Antonio,
Tex.: The Naylor Company, 1942), pp. 246-47.

A Mr. George Shears approached the gallows with this comment: "Gentlemen, I am not used to this business, having never been hung before. Do I jump off or slide off?"[8]

There is a story of a certain "Lame Johnny" whose only claim to immortality was a mouth big enough to plop a cantaloupe into. Lame Johnny made the mistake of stealing a horse, was caught, and toted off to Boot Hill. Someone in the group felt that even a horse thief should have an epitaph, and finally one grizzled old cowman came up with this:

"Lame Johnny"
Stranger, pass gently over this sod.
If he opens his mouth, you're gone, by God!

Fly-Speck Bill, horse thief and murderer, was introduced to a vigilante's rope one bitterly cold winter night. The committee, fearing trouble with the law, was at the coroner's the next morning and asked if he would be so kind as to square things when he made his report.

"Well, I don't know, boys," the coroner replied. "Did you leave Bill hangin' there in that tree all night?"

"Yup."

"That being the case," said the coroner, "Old

---

[8] Rollins, *loc. cit.*

Bill sure would have frozen to death if he hadn't got his neck busted. I reckon I'll jes' have to report he died from 'overexposure.' "

Another coroner performed "assessment work" on the remains of a badly shot-up gentleman and found that the body was "rich in lead but too badly punctured to hold whisky."[9]

Other outstanding verdicts by coroners are:

". . . came to his death from emphysema of the lungs, which might have been, and probably was, caused by strangulation, self-inflicted or otherwise."[10]

". . . came to his death by suicide. He tried to shoot to death at the distance of a hundred and fifty yards a man armed with a Winchester rifle."[11]

And upon finding the bones of a dead Mexican, Judge Bean noted the bullet hole in the center of the forehead and declared that "this gent met his death at the hands of a doggoned good pistol shot."[12]

[9] Walter Noble Burns, *Tombstone, an Iliad of the Southwest* (Garden City, N.Y.: Doubleday, Page & Company, 1927), pp. 38-39.

[10] Raymond Hatfield Gardner and B. H. Monroe, *The Old Wild West; Adventures of Arizona Bill* (San Antonio, Tex.: The Naylor Company, 1944), p. 77.

[11] Based on a story by Mody C. Boatright, *op. cit.*, p. 19.

[12] Based on a story told by Everett Lloyd in *Law West of the Pecos, the Story of Roy Bean* (San Antonio, Tex.: The Naylor Company, 1936), p. 129. This has been attributed to Judge Roy Bean.

A cowboy once made the mistake of arguing with a trapper over whether wildcats had long tails or not. The trapper settled the argument by furnishing as his proof a Colt .45 revolver. The coroner's decision was that any *hombre* who was crazy enough to call a long-haired, whisky-drinking trapper a liar had, in a strong sense, died of ignorance.

One braggart cowboy loved to flash his gun by twirling it by the trigger guard, a practice which resulted in the accidental death of two people. One night the man disappeared and was next seen hanging from a cottonwood limb with a note from the vigilantes: "This is no accident!"[13]

Another undesirable was found in a similar position. His placard read, "In some ways, this is a very bad man. In other ways, he is a heckava lot worse!"[14]

A railroad bridge once collapsed near Langtry, Texas, killing seven men who were working on it and seriously injuring three others. When Judge Bean arrived on the scene all ten were laid out in a row, and he pronounced them all dead.

---

[13] Miguel Antonio Otero, *My Life on the Frontier, 1864-1882; Incidents and Characters of the Period when Kansas, Colorado, and New Mexico Were Passing through the Last of their Wild and Romantic Years* (New York: The Press of the Pioneers, Incorporated, 1935), p. 193.

[14] Based on a story by Mody C. Boatright, *op. cit.*, p. 162.

"But, Judge!" objected a member of the coroner's jury. "Three of them fellers ain't dead yet!"

"They're close enough to it," replied the judge. "Fifteen miles out here and fifteen miles back is too far to ride jes' to hold another inquest. Them fellers is dead, *legally.*"

One of the victims spent three days of unlawful living before he died in favor of the judge's decision.[15]

While there were actually few lilies among the cowboy breed, there is a distinction to be made between the real and the false tough ones. Some cowboys tried to put on a big show for tenderfeet, and some even learned stereotyped Western brags that would impress the uninitiated. The recital would go something like this:

"I'm the baddest of the bad men from Bitter Creek. I sleep in a den of live rattlesnakes an' I live on the blood of mountain lions. The farther up Bitter Creek yuh goes, the meaner people gits, an' I live at the headwaters."[16]

---

[15] Boyce House, *Cowtown Columnist* (San Antonio, Tex.: The Naylor Company, 1946), p. 37.

[16] Variations of this type of braggadocio are given by Rollins in *The Cowboy;* by Edgar Rye in *The Quirt and the Spur; Vanishing Shadows of the Texas Frontier* (Chicago: W. B. Conkey Company [c. 1909]); and by Boatright in *Folk Laughter on the American Frontier.*

Similar to this is the story of the man who arrived in Arkansas driving a two-wheeled cart which was drawn by a pair of mountain lions. The man was unkempt and bearded, wore two big six-shooters around his waist, and had a bowie knife stuck in his belt. On the seat beside him rode a snarling wildcat and, for a whip, the stranger used a live rattlesnake. After he had ordered and drunk a gallon of sulfuric acid, this woolly *hombre* was asked to tell where he came from.

"Oklahomy," he said, wiping his mouth with the back of his hand. "Things're gettin' so bad in there that all us sissies are havin' to get out!"[17]

But the West did not care for braggarts, as is evident in the cowboy's humor of story and ballad. One yarn, for instance, tells of the waddie who decided to show off his toughness. Buckling on his hardware, he downed some "bravemaker" and started out. First he raced his horse up and down the street firing off his gun and yelling; then he swaggered into the saloon chanting a boast which he had memorized.

He shouted, "I wear .45's on both hips and carry a .44 jes' fer to pick my teeth. I use a

<hr />

[17] Edward Everett Dale, *Cow Country* (Norman, Okla.: University of Oklahoma Press, 1945) , pp. 140-41.

cactus fer a piller, an' I'm a bad man to monkey with! I'm a wild and woolly wolf!"

About that time the marshal, who had been sitting quietly to one side, came up and said:

"So you're a wolf, huh?"

"Tha's right. A wolf!"

The marshal drew himself up and looked the other square in the eye. "Jes' what sort of wolf are you?"

"Aw," said the waddie, "I'm jes' a little ol' coyote."[18]

In his *Cowboy Lingo*, Ramon F. Adams records this classic description of a would-be bad man:

. . . This old catawampus comes rackin' to town an' orates as how he's got more troubles than a rat-tailed hoss tied short in fly-time. He proceeds to guzzle snake pizen an' hell 'round town until he's knockin' about like a blind dog in a meat shop. He tries to make it appear he's as tough as tripe an' lets out a yell that'd drive a wolf to suicide. He's standin' on the high gallery of the Silver Spur Saloon when the city marshal swoops down on 'im like forty hen-hawks on a settin' quail, and he pronto gets as harmless as a pet rabbit. He starts to bowin' and bendin' to the law like a pig over a nut, but he loses his balance an' falls down the steps, boundin' 'long like a barrel downhill. When he hits bottom, he begins feelin' over his carcass for broken bones, an' when he don't find none, he heaves such a sigh y'u could feel the draft, but he's considerable

---

[18] Based on a story by Mody C. Boatright, *op. cit.*, pp. 29-31.

He proceeds to guzzle snake pizen and hell 'round town.

sobered. I never laughed so much since I wore three-cornered pants.[19]

Also, there is told the story of the bad man who invaded a cowtown with talk of how he was going to shoot up a certain Vic Smith, famous gunman of the northwestern range areas. His barroom audience listened to him without comment. Then someone stuck his head in the door and called them a "Hello!" Whereupon one of the cowboys called back:

"Why, hulloa, Vic Smith. We 'uz just talkin' about you!"

"Vic Smith!" the stranger howled. "My gawd! I thought he was in Wyoming!" And he disappeared through a window.[20]

In the frontier ballad, "Buckskin Joe," another braggart by the name of Hankey Dean takes great pains to recite his reputation to a mild little fellow with whom he is playing cards.

"Look here, little stranger, do you know who I am?"
"Yes, and I don't care a copper-colored damn!"
The dealers stopped their dealing, and the players held
     their breath,
For words like those to Hankey were a sudden flirt with
     death.

---

[19] Ramon F. Adams, *Cowboy Lingo* (Boston: Houghton Mifflin Company, 1936), pp. 236-37.

[20] Rollins, *op. cit.*, pp. 50-51.

Then Hankey describes to the little man how rattlesnakes have bitten him and crawled off to die, and then he tells of his exploit of cleaning out a den of mountain lions. But the little stranger's only reply is to pull out his "life preserver" and shoot out the spots of the five of spades.

Then Hankey stepped up to the stranger and made a
    neat apology:
"Why—the lions in the mountains—that was nothing
    but a joke.
Never mind about the extra, you are a bad shooting
    man,
And I'm a meek little child and as harmless as a lamb."[21]

A Texas cowboy was asked how many Indians he had killed. He answered that perhaps he had killed one, and when pressed for the gruesome details explained that once some Indians had been chasing him and that he was practically certain one had become overheated and died of a bad cold.[22]

Not all of the woolly ones, however, were so modest. John Wesley Hardin bet a glass of beer that he could make a man jump ten feet by shooting close to him, did, and won the beer. Clay

---

[21] John A. Lomax, *Cowboy Songs and Other Frontier Ballads* (New York: The Macmillan Company, 1925), pp. 171-72.

[22] Based on a story told by W. S. James in *Cowboy Life in Texas,* p. 164, as quoted by Boatright, *op. cit.,* pp. 57-58.

Allison, of New Mexico, went to a dentist to get a tooth pulled. The dentist pulled the wrong one, whereupon Clay went back, hit the dentist over the head with the butt of his revolver, and drew six teeth in revenge.[23]

A cowboy rode into a Tascosa, Texas, dance hall and proceeded to shoot the place up. Then he rode out the back door and around again to the front. This time the proprietor was waiting for him with a shotgun.

"You'll pass here only over my dead body," announced the dance hall owner.

"That's easy," agreed the cowboy, and shot him dead.[24]

Faro Nell had just shot a man in a saloon quarrel; then, for good measure, she ran the bartender out of the saloon. All this accomplished, she toed the corpse and made a statement for her public.

"I allus knew I 'uz gonna have trouble with this coyote," said she. "Jes' look at the shape of his head."[25]

A cowboy had rented a hotel room and, because of crowded conditions, was forced to share

---

[23] Gardner and Monroe, *op. cit.,* p. 97.

[24] William MacLeod Raine, *Guns on the Frontier; The Story of How Law Came to the West* (Cleveland: World Publishing Co., 1940) , p. 125.

[25] Gardner and Monroe, *op. cit.,* p. 113.

it with another guest. It turned out to be a big, fat man who came into the room and started to undress. The cowboy remarked that he was subject to fits and liable to have one any time and hoped that he would not be a bother. Actually he was wishing, of course, that the big man would decide to get another room. Instead, the other tucked his six gun carefully under his pillow and said, "That's all right. I've got a sure cure for fits." He went to sleep, and so did the cowboy who wasn't bothered by a single fit all night.[26]

Another bewhiskered Westerner approached a friend and asked, "Didn't you tell me that Pete Adams called me a hotheaded, overbearing son-of-a-gun?"

"Naw, I never said that."

"Doggone! I've gone and killed an innocent man!"[27]

Naturally there were a good many young boys who were enraptured by the tales of renowned gunmen and Western heroes. Such a person is the hero of a cowboy song called:

---

[26] N. Howard (Jack) Thorp, as told to Neil M. Clark, *Pardner of the Wind* (Caldwell, Idaho: The Caxton Printers, Ltd., 1945), p. 201.

[27] Based on a story by Mody C. Boatright, *op. cit.*, p. 18.

THE LAVENDER COWBOY

He was only a lavender cowboy,
The hairs on his chest were two.
He wanted to follow the heroes
To do as the he-men do.

But he was inwardly troubled
By dreams that gave him no rest:
When he heard of heroes in action
He wanted more hairs on his chest.

Herpicide and many hair tonics
He rubbed in morning and night,
But when he looked into the mirror,
No new hairs grew in sight.

He battled for Red Nellie's honor,
And cleaned out a holdup nest.
He died with his six gun a-smokin'
But only two hairs on his chest![28]

---

[28] Lomax, *op. cit.*, pp. 304-5.

Chapter VI

Cowboy vs. Railroader

*A famous outlaw whose specialty was
train holdups once wrote the Union
Pacific and complained that they
were running their trains entirely too
fast for public convenience.*[1]

ONE OF THE most interesting and certainly the
most amusing rivalries to develop in the old Wild
West was that between the cowboy and the railroader. From the first time a sudden blast of a

---

[1] Philip Ashton Rollins, *The Cowboy, His Characteristics, His
Equipment, and His Part in the Development of the West* (Reprint
ed.; New York: Charles Scribner's Sons, 1936), p. 332.

train whistle caused a range-wild cayuse to toss its rider unceremoniously from its back, the feud was on; and there began the liveliest barrage of insults, sarcastic wit, and funmaking in the history of the West.

To the cowboy, all railroaders were bullheaded Irishmen who took fiendish delight in stampeding herds of cattle. The railroader, on the other hand, viewed cowboys as irresponsible troublemakers who were constantly stringing their herds across the tracks merely to disrupt the railroad's all-important time schedule. Generally, both opinions were entirely correct.

The thing which caused more to-do between the men of these two professions than anything else was the matter of cattle which were hit and killed by trains. The cattleman always claimed the loss to be nothing less than a head of prime beef, while the railroad agent swore in rebuttal that the cowman had placed salt on the tracks so as to lure some of his market-rejected cattle into the path of the train in an attempt to collect from the railroad.

Despite the fact that the railroad was vital in making cattle raising a profitable business by connecting it with the Eastern markets, the cowboy blamed it for the immigration of settlers and homesteaders into areas which he felt were, by

destiny, cattle land. Further, the railroad symbol-
ized change and progress, a couple of items for
which the old-time cowboy had absolutely no use.

Deserved or not, the railroad bore the brunt
of much cowboy sarcasm. The story is told of
an old ranchman who had been the sole eyewitness
to a serious train wreck in the Southwest. He
was called upon by an investigating committee to
give his account of the affair. The rancher's story
went like this:

"Wal, I 'uz ridin' along the backbone of a
ridge lookin' fer mavericks when I saw down to
the south a train comin' along about fifty miles
an hour. Then I looked north and spied another
comin' south at about the same speed, an' I saw
they 'uz goin' ter smack into one another at that
curve."

"What did you do then?"

"Do? Why, nothin'."

"You mean you didn't even try to stop them?"

"No."

"Good lord, man! What were you thinking
about?"

"Wal, fer one thing, I 'uz thinkin' what a heck
uv a way to run a railroad that 'uz!"[2]

Many cowboys, in fact, were firmly convinced

[2] Edward Everett Dale, *Cow Country* (Norman, Okla.: University of Oklahoma Press, 1945), pp. 145-46.

that they were better railroaders than the railroaders. Prairie philosophers spent much of their
time in dreaming up suggestions and new laws
which would stop engines from stampeding horses
and waking people in the middle of the night
with their whistles and bells. One agent, finally
having all this he could stand, wrote to a newspaper with his railroader's sarcasm and suggested
a law of his own: "Whereas any engineer whose
train has frightened a horse will stop immediately, take his engine completely apart, and hide
it in a near-by ditch until the horse has gone on."[3]

Railroaders seldom passed up their opportunities to get back at the men of the cow country.
Accordingly, an engineer of a train loaded with
cattle, aware that the foreman in charge had never
before been aboard a train, began whipping his
cinder wagon around the curves as if it were a
blacksnake. The conductor of the train knew
what was up and kept a close eye on the perspir-
ing waddie. When the ears of the foreman had
taken on a slightly greenish color, the railroader
inquired innocently if they were going too fast
for him.

"Heck, yes!" the cowboy exploded. "I don't
know about the gent that's herdin' this thing,

[3] James Leslie Marshall, *Santa Fe, the Railroad that Built an
Empire* (New York: Random House, Inc., 1945), p. 54.

but personally I'd ruther get to Kansas City an hour late than to get to Hades on time!"[4]

Cowboys had little understanding or sympathy for train rules and generally did their best to break all of them. One waddie, while riding a train which had no diner, decided he was hungry. During a stop he climbed off and came back with a package. Shortly thereafter the conductor saw smoke pouring out of the car. Thinking the train was on fire, he dashed in to help save the passengers. But he discovered that the only thing burning was the steak which the waddie was cooking on top of the train's coal stove. The conductor grabbed the steak and tossed it out the car window, losing forever any chance of friendship with one very disgruntled and still-hungry cow poke.[5]

Another waddie, on his way to visit his girl friend, had bought himself a fancy outfit just before embarking on his journey. In those days there was no men's lounge and, notwithstanding the fact that there were ladies aboard, he proceeded to strip to his long handles and change attire then and there in the parlor car. He prac-

---

[4] Neil M. Clark, "God's Roundup," *Saturday Evening Post,* March 6, 1943, p. 28.

[5] Con Price, *Memories of Old Montana* (Pasadena, Calif.: Trail's End Publishing Co., 1945), pp. 33-34.

tically had to fight the entire train crew, but eventually he managed to get his new suit on and left the train with firm convictions about a railroad that would try to keep him from impressing his lady friend.[6]

The waddie who best expressed the cowboy's sentiment was tobacco-chawing Bill Jones who was making a trip on a stock train. Bill was riding in the caboose, which was equipped with a cuspidor even though Bill evidenced no real ambition to use it, merely snap-shooting in its general direction. When the conductor came in and viewed the results of Bill's tobacco, he angrily demanded that Bill use more caution in aiming at the spittoon. When he was gone Bill loosed another barrage, this time with bull's-eye accuracy.

"That's jes' the way with them dern railroaders," he commented bitterly. "Gettin' more doggoned p'tickler all the time!"[7]

Train riding to most cowboys, at least for the first time, was an adventure and quite often a hilarious one. No better comedy has come out of the West than is to be found in Colonel Jack Potter's account of his first train ride which appeared in *The Trail Drivers of Texas*. In the spring of 1882, Potter made his first trail drive to

---

[6] *Loc. cit.*
[7] Dale, *op. cit.*, pp. 19-20.

Colorado. The drive up was uneventful, with just the usual stampedes and Indian engagements, but the trip back home *via railroad* gave Potter more than his share of trouble.

. . . here I was, a boy not yet seventeen years old, two thousand miles from home. I had never been on a railroad train, had never slept in a hotel, never taken a bath in a bath house, and from babyhood I had heard terrible stories about ticket thieves, money-changers, pickpockets, three-card monte, and other robbing schemes, and I had horrors about this, my first railroad trip. The first thing I did was to make my money safe by tying it up in my shirt tail. I had a draft for $150 and some currency. I purchased a second-hand trunk and about two hundred feet of rope with which to tie it. The contents of the trunk were one apple-horn saddle, a pair of chaps, a Colt's .45, one sugan, a hen-skin blanket, and a change of dirty clothes.

. . . About four p.m. the Union Pacific train came pulling into Greeley. Then it was a hasty handshake with the boys. One of them handed me my trunk check, saying, "Your baggage is loaded. Good-bye, write me when you get home," and the train pulled out. It took several minutes for me to collect myself, and then the conductor came through and called for the tickets. When I handed him my ticket he punched a hole in it, and then pulled out a red slip, punched it, too, and slipped it into my hatband. I jumped to my feet and said, "You can't come that one on me. Give me back my ticket," but he passed out of hearing, and as I had not yet learned how to walk on a moving train, I could not follow him. When I had become fairly settled in my seat again the train crossed a bridge, and as it went by I thought the thing was going to hit me on the head.

I dodged those bridges all the way up to Denver. When I reached there I got off at the Union Station and walked down to the baggage car, and saw them unloading my trunk. I stepped up and said: "I will take my trunk." A man said, "No; we are handling this baggage." "But," said I, "that is my trunk, and has my saddle and gun in it." They paid no attention to me and wheeled the trunk off to the baggage room, but I followed right along, determined that they were not going to put anything over me. Seeing that I was so insistent one of the men asked me for the check. It was wrapped up in my shirt tail, and I went after it, and produced the draft I had been given as wages. He looked at it and said, "This is not your trunk check. Where is your metal check with numbers on it?" Then it began to dawn on me what the darn thing was, and when I produced it and handed it to him, he asked me where I was going. I told him to San Antonio, Texas, if I could get there. I then showed him my letter to the general ticket agent, and he said: "Now, boy, you leave this trunk right here and we will recheck it and you need not bother about it." That sounded bully to me.

. . . The next morning I started out to find the Santa Fe ticket office, where I presented my letter to the head man there. . . . As it was near train time I hunted up the baggage crew and told them I was ready to make another start. I showed them my ticket and asked them about my trunk. They examined it, put on a new check, and gave me one with several numbers on it. I wanted to take the trunk out and put it on the train, but they told me to rest easy and they would put it on. I stood right there until I saw them put it on the train, then I climbed aboard.

This being the second day out, I thought my troubles should be over, but not so, for I couldn't face those bridges. They kept me dodging and fighting my head.

An old gentleman who sat near me said, "Young man, I see by your dress that you are a typical cowboy, and no doubt you can master the worst bronco or rope and tie a steer in less than a minute, but in riding on a railway train you seem to be a novice. Sit down on this seat with your back to the front and those bridges will not bother you." And sure enough it was just as he said.

That night Jack arrived in Dodge City, Kansas, and found the town jammed with other trail drivers, and here he came across Jesse Pressnall who told him that old "Dog Face" Smith and his crew were joining the train.

. . . Old "Dog Face" Smith was a typical Texan, about thirty years of age, with long hair and three months' growth of whiskers. He wore a blue shirt and a red cotton handkerchief around his neck. He had a bright, intelligent face that bore the appearance of a good trail hound, which no doubt was the cause of people calling him "Dog Face."

. . . I will never forget seeing that train come into Dodge City that night. Old "Dog Face" and his bunch were pretty badly frightened, and we had considerable difficulty in getting them aboard. It was about 12:30 when the train pulled out. The conductor came around, and I gave him my cowboy ticket. It was almost as long as your arm, and as he tore off a chunk of it I said: "What authority have you to tear up a man's ticket?" He laughed and said, "You are on my division. I simply tore off one coupon and each conductor between here and San Antonio will tear off one for each division." That sounded all right, but I wondered if that ticket would hold out all the way down.

Everyone seemed to be tired and worn out and the bunch began bedding down. Old "Dog Face" was out of humor, and was the last one to bed down. At about three o'clock our train was sidetracked to let the westbound train pass. This little stop caused the boys to sleep the sounder. Just then the westbound train sped by traveling at the rate of about forty miles an hour, and just as it passed our coach the engineer blew the whistle. Talk about your stampedes! That bunch of sleeping cowboys arose as one man, and started on the run with old "Dog Face" Smith in the lead. I was a little slow in getting off, but fell in with the drags. I had not yet woke up, but thinking I was in a genuine cattle stampede, yelled out, "Circle your leaders and keep up the drags." Just then the leaders circled and ran into the drags, knocking some of us down. They circled again and the new butcher crawled out from under foot and jumped through the window like a frog. Before they could circle back the next time, the train crew pushed in the door and caught old "Dog Face" and soon the bunch quieted down. The conductor was pretty angry and threatened to have us transferred to the freight department and loaded into a stock car.

We had breakfast at Hutchinson, and after eating and were again on our way, speeding through the beautiful farms and thriving towns of Kansas, we organized a kangaroo court and tried the engineer of that westbound train for disturbing the peace of passengers on the eastbound train. We heard testimony all morning, and called in some of the train crew to testify. One of the brakemen said it was an old trick for that engineer to blow the whistle at that particular siding and that he was undoubtedly the cause of a great many stampedes. The jury brought in a verdict of guilty and assessed the death penalty. It was ordered that he be captured, taken to some place on the western trail, there to be hog-tied like a steer, and then have the road brand applied with a good hot iron and a herd of not less than five thousand long-horn Texas steers made to stampede and trample him to death. . . .

. . . Pretty soon the porter called out "San Antonio, Santonnie-o," and that was music to my ears. My first move on getting off the train was to look for my trunk and found it had arrived. I said to myself, "Jack Potter, you're a lucky dog. Ticket held out all right, toe nails all healed up, and trunk came through in good shape."[8]

Of course, cowboys made up a good many jokes about the railroad. A cowboy was supposedly riding a very slow train one time and noticed that every so often the train would come to a stop. The cowboy asked the conductor what was wrong, and the conductor answered that there was a cow on the tracks. Again they moved on very slowly, and again they stopped. Once more the cowboy inquired as to the trouble.

"Oh," said the conductor, "you remember that cow I told you about back there? Well, we caught up with her again."[9]

Another cowboy claimed to be riding a slow train and complained that he could walk faster than the train was moving. The railroader's

---

[8] J. Marvin Hunter (comp. and ed.) *The Trail Drivers of Texas* (2 vols. in 1; Nashville, Tenn.: Cokesbury Press, 1925), pp. 58-71.

[9] Federal Writers' Project, *Idaho Lore*, edited by Vardis Fisher (Caldwell, Idaho: The Caxton Printers, Ltd., 1939), p. 132.

answer was that he could do that also, but the company wouldn't let him.[10]

One of the favorite tricks practiced by cowboys when celebrating was to rope the smokestacks of trains. It was this that probably gave rise to the story of Peckerwood Pete. Pete was a prize roper. He seldom missed with his loop, and his horse, "Straightedge," was a wonderful roping horse. So it wasn't unnatural that when Pete heard that the Texas and Pacific Railroad employed "cow-catchers," he was interested.

Now Pete didn't have any idea exactly what the railroad used cowcatchers for, but he was dead certain that he would make a good one. He rode to town and asked for employment, modestly giving his qualifications as the best cowcatcher in the state of Texas. Pete didn't know it, but he was telling his story to the conductor of the train which had just pulled in. The conductor agreed to give Pete a tryout and suggested he ride up the track about a quarter of a mile and, when the engine came by, show what a good roper he was.

Peckerwood Pete rode with confidence up the track, and by the time the train got even with him it was gaining a pretty good speed. Straight-

_____
[10] *Ibid.*, p. 119.

Pete decided he didn't care much for working on the railroad.

edge was shy as a rabbit of this smoking, clanging object, but Pete finally got him to lay in close. Then, at just the right moment, Pete's loop shot true. Straightedge squatted, the rope held, and the cinches broke. And Pete? Well, Pete decided that he didn't care much about working on the railroad.[11]

Whenever things became dull for a puncher lying around a cowtown, there was always the railroad depot where he could find some sort of deviltry with which to amuse himself. The story is told of a cow poke who rounded up a bunch of old newspapers and lay in wait for a westbound passenger train. When the train pulled to a stop, the cowboy began running up and down the station platform yelling, "Read all about it! Read all about it! Sittin' Bull has busted out!"

The train conductor, always wary of Indian uprisings, came dashing up and demanded excitedly, "Where did he break out at?"

"Up and down the legs an' all over," the cowboy yelled and doubled up on the platform in convulsions of laughter.[12]

On another occasion a railroad office once re-

---

[11] J. Frank Dobie, *A Vaquero of the Brush Country* (New York: Grosset & Dunlap, 1929), pp. 240-41.

[12] Con Price, *Trails I Rode* (Pasadena, Calif.: Trail's End Publishing Co., 1947), p. 95.

ceived a telegram from a trail herd foreman requesting cars in which to ship some 2,500 *sea lions.* Railroad officials were amazed and wired back to the original dispatcher for further clarification of the order. The dispatcher couldn't locate the cowboy who had sent the wire, but another waddie read it over and grinned. He explained that the foreman who had sent the message had probably figured that his cattle had swum so many streams on the way up from Texas that *"sea lions"* was a fit variation of *"sirloin."*[13]

One cowboy who considered himself a tough customer took things too far. He boarded a train one day without a ticket. When the conductor asked him for his fare, the cowboy pulled his six gun and declared that it was all the ticket he needed. The conductor went on his way, but he returned presently with a rifle which he stuck under the cowboy's nose.

"Your ticket has just expired, Mister," he announced and signaled for the train to stop. He let the cowboy off miles from nowhere, and one cowboy learned the advantage of paying his fare before boarding a train.[14]

George W. Saunders liked to spin the yarn

---

[13] Paul I. Wellman, *The Trampling Herd* (New York: Carrick & Evans, Inc., 1939) , p. 119.

[14] Marshall, *op. cit.*, p. 91.

about a Texas cowboy who boarded a train at Denver after having helped in a trail drive to that country.

He walked into the sleeper with a bundle of blankets and asked the Pullman conductor if there was any place where he could bed down. The conductor said sure there was; the cowboy could have either upper or lower. The cowboy said any place would do for him, not knowing what was meant by the upper or lower. The conductor continued, saying: "The lower is higher than the upper. The higher price is for the lower. If you want the lower you will have to go higher. We sell the upper lower than the lower. In other words, the higher the lower. Most people don't like the upper, although it is lower on account of its being higher. When you occupy an upper you have to go up to go to bed, and get down when you get up. You can have the lower if you pay higher. The upper is lower than the lower because its higher. If you are willing to go higher it will be lower." When the conductor looked around the cowboy had spread his blankets down in the aisle of the Pullman, using his boots and pistol for a pillow.[15]

A railroad company once received this letter of complaint from a dissatisfied customer:

DEAR SIR:
6:30 this morning in going to the Stockyards to feed at this place another train run in to my stock train. On an open switch. & killed 2 cows & crippled 4. & the rest of the cows in that car is now all over Town. so I got one car less. & few cows in another car is feeling sore & some of them got one horn left.

---

[15] Hunter, *op. cit.*, pp. 1031-32.

The Crew of both train jumped off & myself. so it was no one hurt. It was not enough left of the engine & one stock car to tell the Fait. 8 or 10 of the Kansas cowboys is all over Town picking up our Cattle—wish you could see them coming down the street driving one or two of them cows—I think they got about 10 of the cows in a Pen (down in Town) & they heard of 5 cows in a corn-field just a little while ago, so I guess they will get most of them back today. I will leave here about 5 P.M. will make tomorrow market.

Yours truly,
Dock.

P.S.—This R.R. ought to take charge of this whole shipment and Pay for same.

P.S.—The Sheriff shot one cow on the street just a little while ago.

P.S.—The cows down in town is making the horses run off with buggys and running all the women out of town.

P.S.—I think this will cost the R.R. a good deal in this town.

P.S.—The Rail Road they give me poor and sorry run.

P.S.—They run my cattle 40 hours before this happened without feed— (how about that).[16]

There were times, of course, when the cowboy-railroader feud was carried on physically as well as verbally. Some old-timers claim they can recall occasions when railroad trains left cowtowns with hot lead pouring back and forth. Generally, though, it was a battle to the last salty comeback.

---

[16] Jules Verne Allen, *Cowboy Lore* (San Antonio, Tex.: The Naylor Printing Company, 1933), pp. 18-19.

Chapter VII

Grub Pi-ii-ile!

*The old-time wagon cook loved to tell
the tenderfoot his favorite recipe for
making cowboy coffee. With the greatest of secrecy he would say: "Take two
pounds of Arbuckle's, put in 'nough
water to wet it down, boil for two
hours, and then throw in a hoss shoe.
If the hoss shoe sinks, she ain't ready."*[1]

So GOES THE famous old prescription of the men
of the open range who reputedly spent most of

---

[1] Ramon F. Adams, *Western Words: A Dictionary of the Range,
Cow Camp and Trail* (Norman: University of Oklahoma Press,
1945) , p. 6.

their natural lives in a state of hunger. It was their belief that the best seasoning for any food was a salty sense of humor. Humoring the daily bread was a time-honored custom for cowboys, whether at home quarters, on the range, or off trail in some fancy city restaurant. One cowboy on a visit to town saw a sign reading:

> Snack—two bits
> Square meal—four bits
> Bellyache—one dollar![2]

He entered the establishment and, when the waitress came up, ordered a dozen rotten eggs and some weak coffee. The waitress thought he was crazy, but the waddie explained that he had a tapeworm and he'd be doggoned if he was going to feed it first-class chuck.

The first stop for a cowboy in town was generally the saloon, but once he had washed the dust from his throat he was likely to head for the closest restaurant to fill up on the luxury of either eggs or steak or both. Chickens were scarce on the range, and eggs were the one thing which the West admitted the East topped it in.[3] Many a cafe "biscuit shooter," upon seeing a

---

[2] Philip Ashton Rollins, *The Cowboy, His Characteristics, His Equipment, and His Part in the Development of the West* (Reprint ed.; New York: Charles Scribner's Sons, 1936), p. 324.

[3] *Ibid.*, 164.

cowboy crew hit town, would dig out all of his "states fruit" even before he heard the inevitable "Keep mine bright-eyed," or "I'll have 'em dirty on both sides."

Cowboys generally liked their meat well done, and the old cow hand who bowlegged his way into an El Paso restaurant was no exception. He ordered a big steak, telling the waitress he wanted it well done. But when she brought it, the meat was anything but burned. The cowboy asked her to take it back to be cooked some more, but she insisted that the steak was done.

"Done, heck!" exploded the old cowboy. "Out where I come from, cows have been hurt worse than that an' got well!"[4]

Another puncher was told that the eating hours at a certain hotel restaurant were from twelve to three. He was astounded that it took the town folks three hours to fill up, but he followed the custom. He ate for three hours and announced afterwards that he felt sort of "satisfied and fixed up for business."

Even further significance was attached to the matter of eating through the role played by the chuck wagon in range work. The wagon was the

---

[4] Frank M. King, *Wranglin' the Past* (Pasadena, Calif.: Trail's End Publishing Co., 1935), p. 97.

central hub of all range activity, the meeting place for cowboys during roundups and trail drives, and the storage place for clean clothes, valuables, and equipment. Captain of this cow country institution was the cook, better known as the dough-roller, grub-wrangler, biscuit-shooter, cookie, and various other cowboy-coined titles.

The average ranch cook was generally a waddie who was too stove up to capably handle his range duties, and all his culinary training had previously been done atop a bucking bronc. Some noted range cooks, however, were in their own rights chefs of the first order, considering what they had to work with. From their chuck-wagon kitchens came such famous dishes as sowbelly (bacon) and beans, son-of-a-gun stew, frying-pan bread, and other Western delicacies.

Because of this the cook was accorded a certain reverence and respect in cow-camp society. He was ruler supreme of the grub box, and allotted to him was the special privilege of being as cranky and bullheaded as he wished—as long as he produced good grub. But for anyone but the foreman to criticize seriously one's own dough-roller was to court trouble. A cowboy, who was well aware of this, forgot himself once and blurted out a gripe that the biscuits were burned, then remembered and saved himself by adding: "But, doggone, I sure like 'em that way."[5]

The cook of one outfit had a reputation for being of a mean disposition and for demanding that the men eat what he prepared. And, as one waddie put it, he would "jes' bog down a few raisins in dough and call 'er puddin'."[6] One waddie from another outfit dropped by the ranch early one morning and was invited to sit in at chuck.

The menu was flapjacks, and the cowboy downed the first stack in fine shape. The next bunch went slower, but the waddie, remembering stories he had heard of how mean this cookie could get, ate them all. When he had finished, he was amazed to see the cook bringing in another batch. The cowboy was stuffed, yet he feared that if he refused them he might stir up the cook's temper. Finally, with the help of two cups of coffee, he managed to force them down, aware all the time that the cook was glowering at him from the door of the kitchen. The cowboy had just started to rise when the cookie stomped in and slammed down another platter of hotcakes in front of the waddie.

"Here's some more," the cook snapped, "but

---

[5] Rollins, *op. cit.*, p. 66.

[6] Ramon F. Adams, *Cowboy Lingo* (Boston: Houghton Mifflin Company, 1936), p. 149.

The cookie wasn't noted for his smilin' disposition.

I'll go t' Hades afore I'll mix another batch. I never saw such a derned hog in all my life!"

A lady tenderfoot once complained that a certain cook didn't even wash his hands when he baked bread. The cook overheard the remark and was very indignant.

"Why, sure I do!" he replied. "How'd I ever get the dough offen 'em if I didn't?"[7]

There were a good many jokes told about cooks. One is the story of the two cowboys who visited a chuck wagon one day while the cook was gone. Being hungry, they proceeded to dig some food out of the chuck box. After eating, they decided to play a joke on the cook by burning a "WE8" (we ate) brand in the seat of the cookie's extra breeches. When they had gone, another cow hand drifted in and helped himself to a free meal. As he was eating, he noticed the pants and, before he left, added another brand: "ME2."

Now, it was a common practice on the range for visitors to help themselves to the food at whatever ranch house, line camp, or chuck wagon they visited. The only requirement was for them to wash the dishes when they were through. But when this cook returned and found the messages

across the seat of his pants, he felt that the limits
of hospitality had been crossed. He took out after
the cowboys, caught them one by one, and tied
them, feet and other parts up, to a tree. Then,
supposedly without removing the wearing apparel,
he proceeded to make a brand of his own. "YY"
in cowboy lingo means "too wise," and the cook's
brand was "3YY."[8]

It was the cook's place to choose the camping
spot on the range, and he did so with two factors
in mind: forage for the horses, and drinking
water. Sometimes the cookie would have to drag
the carcass of a steer from the water hole, and
sometimes the hole would be rimmed by the tell-
tale white of alkali. It was during a stop at such
a place that a waddie rode up to the wagon and
took a drink of water. The water was hot and
tasted strongly of alkali. The cowboy was thirsty
and swallowed the liquid but, afterwards, he complained of its strongness.

"Shucks!" the cook answered disgustedly. "Yuh
didn't even chaw it afore yuh swallered it."

On another occasion a waddie from another
ranch was joining a crew in chuck. The menu
was slumgullion, and it was mixed generously

[8] Oren Arnold and John P. Hale, *Hot Irons: Heraldry of the Range* (New York: The Macmillan Company, 1940), p. 215, as told by S. Omar Barker.

with grains of sand. The home crew could not complain, but the visiting cowboy was under no such restraint. He inquired if someone had by mistake emptied his boot over the food.

"Look," the cookie said, "don't you know that the Good Book says that we all have to eat a peck of dirt in our lifetime?"

"Sure," the waddie answered. "But derned if I want to eat the hull peck at once!"

Cooks on trail drives were quite often pestered a good deal by Indians over whose lands they had to travel, and who came up to the chuck wagon and demanded food. One hash slinger had had his fill of this and, when the next Indian buck came up, he loaded the customer with dried apples, which he had salted heavily. When the Indian had gone, the cookie doubled up in laughter at what he figured would happen when his visitor reached water and drank his fill.[9]

Range cook Jack Martin was an outstanding character, as range cooks generally were. Jack's cooking was fine, but his drinking was even better. One day the foreman returned to find him drunk, with no food ready for the crew. The foreman was pretty upset about the matter and let Jack

—————
[9] As told by R. J. (Bob) Lauderdale and John M. Doak in *Life on the Range and on the Trail*, edited by Lela Neal Pirtle (San Antonio, Tex.: The Naylor Company, 1936), pp. 18-19.

know in no polite terms exactly what he thought of the situation.

"Wal, what do you want me to cook?" asked Jack.

The question put the foreman in foreign territory.

"Oh, just a little of everything," he said and went back to work. When the crew came in for noon chow, Jack had one pot on the campfire. It was filled with a conglomeration of food—beans, rice, beef, currants—"Jest a little of everything," Jack explained.[10]

At another cow camp the menu became so monotonous that the crew threatened to kill the cook unless he made a change. That night the cook rode to town and made a purchase. The next morning the crew was greeted with a newfangled concoction called "Jello." The boys had to eat it because there was nothing else. When the meal was over, the cook asked one of the crew how he liked the meal.

"Heck," the waddie grumbled. "I'd just as soon put a funnel in my mouth and run against the wind."[11]

---

[10] J. Evetts Haley, *George W. Littlefield, Texan* (Norman, Okla.: University of Oklahoma Press, 1943), pp. 115-16.

[11] Arnold and Hale, *op. cit.*, p. 210.

Uncle Ike Hubbard was once eating supper at a roundup wagon and was purposely doing an artistic job of complaining about the chow. Finally he got under the skin of the cook, who asked with sarcastic sweetness:

"Do you think yuh kin manage to eat them biscuits, Uncle Ike, or shall I toss 'em out and try makin' a new batch?"

"Oh, they ain't so bad," answered Uncle Ike. "That is, if you put a lot o' this butter on 'em so you can't taste 'em quite so much. Course you kin still taste the butter, but then I'm purty strong, as th' feller said, an' anyhow your coffee is weak enough to bring up the general average."[12]

Often a good deal of rivalry existed between cowboys of different states. On one occasion the crew of a Texas trail herd was dining in the house of a grizzled Montana rancher. One of the dishes of the meal was a heaping platter of carrots. When they came to one Texas cowpuncher, the waddie pushed back the carrots with a disgusted face and commented that down in Texas they fed such food to hogs. The Montanan looked up from his plate and shoved the platter back toward the Texan.

"So do we," he said. "Have some."

_____
[12] Edward Everett Dale, *Cow Country* (Norman, Okla.: University of Oklahoma Press, 1945), pp. 144-45.

Two cowboys, Solemn and Squatty, were in the big city, but they had only fifty cents between them. They had just delivered six carloads of horses and had not had time to "fancy up" any. Instead of their usual sweet selves, they looked more like a pair of real, woolly outlaws. Despite their state of near poverty, they entered a large restaurant and ordered a big meal. As they were eating, Solemn remarked casually, though in a carrying voice:

"Don't yuh think I done right, Squatty, to shoot that restaurant man last night?"

"You couldn't hardly a done nothin' else," Squatty agreed.

They ate their meal and ordered a second round. Between courses, Solemn idly twirled the cylinder of his six gun.

"Thet feller didn't treat us right."

"Yup! He was meaner'n a sidewinder in a hot skillet."

The restaurant man asked if they would have anything else. Solemn said he believed he would have a pie, and Squatty agreed.

"That there feller brought his troubles on hisself," Solemn remarked over the coffee which followed the pie. "Imagine him tryin' to charge us more'n a quarter jes' fer one meal!"

"Yup. He brung it on hisself."

The punchers topped off the meal with a good cigar each, then asked the restaurant man how much they owed him.

"W-would twenty cents be about right?"[13]

Two other punchers were on a trip into Canada and had to make a long ride back without water. The weather was very warm and so, on the morning of their return trip, cowboy Bill told his partner not to put too much salt in their food. But the other was out of sorts that morning and said that he wanted plenty of salt—water or no water. All their food was in one frying pan, so Bill took a knife and ran a line through the grub, telling his partner to keep salt off of his half of the food. This made the other pretty angry, and so he put all the more salt on his own half of the frying pan.

Bill's favorite story after that was to tell how his partner nearly choked to death for water that day and how, when they finally reached a river, instead of stooping down to get water his partner ran right on into the river so that he could drink standing up.[14]

---

[13] N. Howard (Jack) Thorp, as told to Neil M. Clark, *Pardner of the Wind* (Caldwell, Idaho: The Caxton Printers, Ltd., 1945), pp. 211-12. An adaptation.

[14] Con Price, *Memories of Old Montana* (Pasadena, Calif.: Trail's End Publishing Co., 1945), p. 80.

A favorite joke of Con Price, Charlie Russell's good friend, is about an old man who operated a little grocery store close to where Price's outfit was once camped. Near by was a boardinghouse, managed by an elderly Irish woman. In those days it was hard to get white sugar most of the time, and brown sugar was used instead. The brown sugar came in barrels and, when the weather was rainy, it would draw moisture, becoming quite heavy. And each time the old lady bought sugar she would accuse the old man of putting water in it to make it weigh more.

One morning the old man saw her coming and quickly got a bucket of water. When she came into the store, he was standing near the barrel with the bucket in his hand. The old woman ran up to him and waved her fist in his face.

"Aha!" she said. "I've caught you this time. I knew you were watering that sugar!"

After that the old lady never had another word to say about the matter, seeming perfectly contented now that she had proved her suspicions of the storekeeper.[15]

The story is told that at a ranch one Sunday they were enjoying the delicacy of fried chicken. Unfortunately, the platter started at the far end

_____
[15] *Ibid.,* p. 16.

of the table from a certain waddie who was forced to watch the best parts of the chicken disappear rapidly. As a fork stabbed into the last drumstick, the cowboy cursed in disgust.

"What'sa matter, Tom?" the owner of the fork asked innocently. "Don't yuh like chicken?"

"Oh, sure," Tom answered with deep sarcasm. "Jes' pass me down some of th' feathers."

Another story tells of a rambunctious old Texas rancher who made a lot of money and decided to crash the social world. But this rancher had a young son who was constantly getting into scrapes of some sort, and the old man tried hard to teach him some manners. Everything went along fine for a while, and the rancher decided to hold a big party in honor of the boy. He had the ranch fixed up until it looked like a funeral parlor on the day that the mayor was buried. He invited the wealthiest and best-known families in that part of Texas.

The boy's debut was a big success until, during the dinner, someone made an insulting remark about the young gentleman. Immediately he jumped up and started for the one who had spoken, but the old man grabbed him by the seat of his pants.

"But, Pa!" cried the boy. "You heard what he

called me. You ain't gonna have me let him get away with it, are you?"

"No," the rancher answered. "But put down that knife and use your fork!"[16]

Old Hank Adams was up in the big city one time with money in his pocket and he decided to eat dinner in one of the better restaurants. He was studying the menu, wondering which part of a cow critter was worth four dollars, when he overheard a dude party at the next table giving the waitress their orders.

"I'll have a steak," one of them said. "And I'd like it rare."

"I'll take the same," another told her. "Only make mine very rare."

"A steak, also," said the third member of the group. "But just sear mine on the outside."

Old Hank liked his meat well done, but he couldn't stand to be outstripped by a bunch of dudes.

"That's what I want, too," he hollered to the waitress. "Jes' cripple 'im up a bit and drive 'im on in."[17]

[16] J. Frank Dobie, *The Flavor of Texas* (Dallas, Tex.: Dealey & Lowe, 1936), pp. 6-7.

[17] Dale, *op. cit.*, pp. 141-42.

Two cowboys had been on the trail for some time and had not even so much as seen a jack rabbit for game. They were getting pretty hungry when they spied a turkey gobbler in a tree. They shot it and only then discovered that it was a tame turkey. But, since the bird was pretty dead by that time, they decided that they might as well go ahead and eat it. They had made camp and were cooking the turkey by the time an angry farmer made his appearance. He caught the cowboys with a big hunk of the bird in their mouths, chewing away hungrily. For a moment it looked bad for the waddies. Then one of them waved a drumstick in the air and suggested:

"Squat and dig in, mister. We got more *Meleagris americana* than we can handle by ourselves."

The farmer was overwhelmed and joined them in their feast of turkey, alias *Meleagris americana*.[18]

A cowboy who was noted for his extremely wide mouth and for his ability to stow away chuck listened to his employer brag as to how the new windmill he had brought in was going to revolutionize the cattle industry. The cowboy looked

---

[18] N. A. Jennings, *A Texas Ranger;* foreword by J. Frank Dobie (Dallas, Tex.: Southwest Press [c. 1930]) , pp. 212-15.

at the tiny stream of water which the windmill was sending forth and shook his head.

"Heck," he said. "I could drink water faster'n that thing could throw it out."

A small wager was made and the cowboy began his guzzling. Just then the wind stopped blowing, and the water ceased to flow. The cowboy got up disgustedly.

"It knowed it didn't have a chance," he said and collected his bet.

An anecdote well known through the West at one time came from the dairy which Judge Roy Bean supposedly operated. It seems that once business was so good that Bean was forced to water the milk in order to have enough to go around among his customers. One day a man came to him and said that, if it was all the same to the judge, he'd like to have his milk and water in separate pails.

"Why, what's wrong?" Judge Bean asked innocently. "You don't think that I've been watering my milk, do you?"

"Well," the other answered, "we found a minnow in the milk yesterday."

"Wal, what do you know!" Bean exclaimed.

"That's what comes of waterin' them cows at the creek!"[19]

Another yarn told in Texas for many years concerned Sam Houston, who was dining in some very fancy company. The general reputedly had a very heavy appetite and ate all his food very hurriedly. By mistake he took a great bite of some steaming hot rice and instantly ejected it back into his bowl. He looked up to see that every eye around the table was on him. The general paused:

"Many a dern fool," he observed, "would have swallered that."[20]

---

[19] Based on a story told by C. L. Sonnichsen in *Roy Bean; Law West of the Pecos* (New York: The Macmillan Company, 1943), p. 127.

[20] Dobie, *op. cit.*, pp. 6-7.

Chapter VIII

Pilgrims

When he meets a greener he ain't afraid to rig,
Stands him on a chuck-box and makes him dance a jig.[1]

To THE COWBOY of the nineteenth century there had never been a more humorous creature conceived than the tenderfoot who wandered guilelessly into the West. Formally educated usually, yet completely ignorant of Western ways, the tenderfoot was a ripe target for cowboy humor.

---

[1] N. Howard (Jack) Thorp, as told to Neil M. Clark, *Pardner of the Wind* (Caldwell, Idaho: The Caxton Printers, Ltd., 1945), p. 277.

Partly in defense against Eastern arrogance and partly out of just plain orneriness, the cowboy immediately and wholeheartedly adopted the greenhorn as his favorite play toy. No single subject provided him with more hilarious mirth, and none received more undivided attention.

Especially the Maker must have had tongue in cheek when He first put into an Englishman's head the idea of investing in American cattle. There were undoubtedly few planets in the heavens which could have provided a being less congruous to the West. The Englishman's speech, his manners, his attitudes, his humors were almost opposite to those of the cowboy world. And yet—credit to both the cowboy and the Englishman—many of them molded themselves with British persistency into the pattern and became real folks of the cow country.

A favorite joke concerning the English cousins was about the monocled gentleman who was visiting his first Western ranch. When taken on a tour of the ranch, he was amazed at the size of it, but more so at the number of cattle which were upon it.

"By Jove!" he exclaimed. "And where do you find milkmaids for all of them?"[2]

Another is of the Englishman whom two cow-

---

[2] *Ibid.,* p. 102.

boys found starving for water on the edge of a flowing creek. The creek was surrounded on both sides by arid wasteland, and the day was a hot one. As they approached, the Englishman ran toward them waving his arms wildly. His tongue was so badly parched he could hardly talk.

"My word!" he managed to gasp. "Have either of you good fellows a tin cup about you?"[3]

One of the most amusing stories concerning Englishmen is told by Willie Newbury Lewis in *Between Sun and Sod*. Newly arrived in the West was a young Englishman whose brother was a big rancher in the Texas Panhandle. This young man, it was soon discovered, prided himself on what the cowboys called "high-soundin' oratory." The boy, Vincent by name, began to take an interest in the ranch. One day he discovered that a nester had squatted on a part of his brother's finest land and he was appalled at such a lack of respect for the law. No one else seemed overly concerned about the matter, but the more Vincent meditated the more certain he was that a serious crime was being committed, and that only ignorance could prompt such a deed. He decided, therefore, to take the matter into his own hands.

All that night he worked very hard preparing

---

[3] *Ibid.*, p. 205.

a speech with which he could explain the matter to the nester, even keeping others awake to practice his creation upon them. The next morning, red-eyed but confident, Vincent rode for the nester's shack. The cowboys of the ranch watched him start away with some misgivings, but they decided that this was Vincent's play and it was not for them to interfere.

Vincent found the nester at home and respectfully but firmly delivered his speech, saying in effect: "You can't do this thing. The land is ours by law, and if you willfully appropriate it for personal use you will be taking that to which you have no right, and in doing so you will be desecrating every principle for which our ancestors fought and bled."

Having spoken, Vincent touched his quirt to his horse and rode proudly off.

Next day the cowboys of the ranch were more than surprised to discover that the nester had moved. It remained a mystery until one day one of the cowboys ran across the man and inquired as to why he had moved without putting up a fight. When asked by the others what reason the nester had given, the cowboy answered, "Oh, he didn't give much reason at all. He said that if Vincent's pappy had fought and bled over that piece of land he kind of figgered the kid ought to have it."[4]

The tenderfoot's gullibility was a red flag to the imaginative cowboy, and to him it was generally a matter of art to see just how long he could "string the greener." One old poke was guiding a city-bred group on a camping trip and, upon passing a lake which had dried while others were full, was asked by a lady to explain the phenomenon.

"Lady," he said, "last year a party of Dutchmen camped and fished here, an' caught a lot of fish. They brought plenty of grub along, also beer, and a barrel of pretzels. When they left, they found they had almost a half a barrel of pretzels left, an' not wanting to haul 'em away, they dumped 'em in the lake. That's why that there lake is dry."

"I don't see——"

"Ma'am," the cowboy explained patiently, "the fish ate them pretzels an' got so thirsty that they drank up all the water."[5]

An Eastern lady once inquired of a cowboy guide as to what made him walk so bowlegged.

[4] Willie Newbury Lewis, *Between Sun and Sod* (Clarendon, Tex.: Clarendon Press, 1938), p. 110.

[5] Thorp, *op. cit.*, pp. 201-2.

"Lady," said Joe solemnly, "I've been sittin' astraddle a horse so long that my two legs are practically strangers to each other. When I start to walk, my two legs keep saying to each other, 'You let me by this time and I'll let you by next time!' "[6]

One of the old favorite pranks to pull on unsuspecting pilgrims was the badger fight. The cowboy, by fostering little remarks here and there, would create an air of mystery that would cause the newcomer to itch to know what was going on. Presently he would be told, "Badger fight. Ever see one?"

Of course he hadn't, and the cowboys would take him into their confidence and allow him to watch one that night, provided, of course, that he said nothing about it. Otherwise they might all end up in the *jusgado*. A couple of the boys would round up a fierce-looking dog, and everything would be made ready at some old stable or barn. The badger, which was supposedly kept half-starved under a box, would have to be freed by someone who would upset the box. This privilege was always given to the tenderfoot. When the time came, the wide-eyed and excited "goat"

---

[6] Frank J. Taylor, "Beauts and Saddles," *Colliers,* August 8, 1936, p. 21.

would give a hearty yank on the rope that disappeared under the box and out would come a nice, white bedroom pot. Then the drinks were on the initiated greenhorn.[7]

A favorite joke concerning the ignorance of the Easterner toward the West is about a young fellow who came to New Mexico to regain his failing health. The boy applied for a job with a sheepherder, saying that while he wasn't much of a rider he was pretty fast on his feet. He claimed to have been quite a runner in college.

The sheepherder ordinarily wouldn't have hired him, but he was planning a trip and needed someone to tend his flocks while he was gone. He told the boy that in sheepherding horses were not used, since it was easier to keep them from straying on foot. He hired the tenderfoot, but cautioned him emphatically not to let the sheep stray for he couldn't afford to lose any. The young man promised faithfully.

The sheep rancher made his trip and, upon returning six weeks later, found his hired hand looking well and happy and more robust than ever. When asked how the sheep and he had gotten along, the boy replied that the old sheep had acted all right but that the lambs had been

[7] Thorp, *op. cit.*, p. 205.

unruly. He had been compelled to tie them up to keep them from straying.

The sheepman was amazed for the lambs were the least likely to stray. He went around behind the corral to see the wayward lambs and beheld a sight which staggered him. Tethered out were nearly fifty big jack rabbits! The boy had mistaken them for lambs.[8]

One autumn afternoon several cowboys were sitting on their horses idly watching the passengers alight from a delayed eastbound train. Among them was a college undergraduate, sunny-faced, who inquired the result of a big football game played the previous day and then began to pace up and down the platform. Presently someone from a westbound train called, "Hello, Jim. Congratulations. You beat us yesterday, ten to nothing." The undergraduate emitted an impulsive cry of joy and danced down the platform. He suddenly stopped, for bedlam had begun. Seven cowboys were yelling and shooting from the backs of horses that, no longer sleepy, were plunging and snorting and rushing about.

The undergraduate's train started, and he climbed aboard it. The punchers and their horses

[8] Sam P. Ridings, *The Chisholm Trail; A History of the World's Greatest Cattle Trail* (Guthrie, Okla.: Co-operative Publishing Company [c. 1936]) , pp. 315-16.

relapsed into quietude. A woman from the westbound train asked the cowboys what they had been celebrating and received the answer.

"We don't know, ma'am. A nice-lookin' young feller that was on the other train heard somethin' that pleased him, and took a contract to deliver a lot of noise. He didn't have much time, so us boys tried to help him out."[9]

One of the standard old jokes of the West is that of the Englishman who bought a herd of cattle from a cattleman and was unaware of the fact that the rancher was reselling cows which were being trotted round a small mountain and run through the counting posts several times. In the herd was an old yellow steer, bobtailed and lop-horned, and with a game leg. On the fifteenth time through for the old steer, the Englishman screwed his eyeglass tighter to his eye and said:

"There are more bloody, blarsted, lop-horned, bobtailed, yellow, crippled brutes than anything else, it seems!"[10]

During the early phases of immigration into

---

[9] Philp Ashton Rollins, *The Cowboy, His Characteristics, His Equipment, and His Part in the Development of the West* (Reprint ed.; New York: Charles Scribner's Sons, 1936), p. 56.

[10] "Cowboy Life on a Sidetrack" (As quoted in *A Vaquero of the Brush Country*, J. Frank Dobie [New York: Grosset & Dunlap, 1929], pp. 165-166).

the West, the number of new arrivals was so few as not to cause the cowboy any great worry. He could eventually indoctrinate these men with the customs of the country or, if the outsider refused to fit, make his stay unpleasant enough to require his moving on. But, eventually, the flow of outsiders into the cattle domain, prompted by the government's wholesale opening of grazing lands to settlement, began to cause him real concern. He saw the open ranges being chewed up by the plow, fences cutting across the old trails, and Eastern culture rapidly strangling out his way of life.

But the cowboy's humor, which had never failed him through hard times, did not fail him now. In *Pardner of the Wind,* Jack Thorp lets a cowboy tell how he felt:

. . . I'm jest about as lonesome with this bunch [of newcomers] as old Slabs Tyson said the cowpuncher was who died an' went to heaven. When he got there, all the men folks had dress suits on, their vests cut 'way down to their waistband, an' tails on their coats 'most to their heels. All the women had on lace clothes, an' not much o' them.

Well, the old puncher was jest rigged out regular, and these high-toned folks turned their noses up at him an' wouldn't speak. This went on for some time, till at last one day he saw St. Peter and asked as a special favor if he couldn't get a pass to go down to hell for a few days and see some of the boys, as there wasn't anybody where he was that he was acquainted with. As he'd behaved pretty well, St. Peter gave him a round-trip ticket good for a week, and off he goes.

Well, the very first person he met after he arrived was an old puncher from his home town, who takes an' leads him aroun' an' shows him the sights. Presently they come to an old barn, an' goin' in there, they sees about a thousand people all settin' 'round. They had candles stuck in old bottles and all of 'em was a-playin' poker; some of 'em the puncher did know and some he didn't.

Pretty soon the old feelin' come over him, an' he jest got to itchin' to horn in, especially when he seen what a little some of 'em did know about the national game. As he didn't have any money, and all the boys he knew seemed 'bout broke, he was in a terrible fix. But at last, after gunnin' 'round among the different players, he noticed a feller that was dressed up fit to kill, and seemed kind of out o' place in that bunch, though he sure had a swell stack o' chips in front of him. The puncher got to talkin' to the dude, an' told about gettin' a ticket from St. Peter, good fer a week, an' after then he'd have to return to heaven. One word brought on another, till at last he swapped his return ticket to heaven for the dude's pile o' chips, sayin' he'd rather live in hell with a bunch o' punchers than in heaven with them damn high-toned dudes.[11]

While the heavenly cowboys might have been content to edge down the bench a ways from greenhorns, there was one old New Mexico bar-dog, a stove-up former cowpuncher, who wasn't quite so congenial about the matter. Several

---

[11] Thorp, *op. cit.*, 214-15.

young punchers rode their horses into his saloon one night and proceeded to wreck the place. During the fracas, an over-dressed drummer from the East got jostled around a bit. The drummer complained bitterly to the bartender, but the old boy just glared right back at him and demanded:

"Jes' what th' heck you doin' in here afoot, anyhow?"[12]

Another yarn of this nature concerns a tenderfoot who stopped in at a western saloon where a card game was in progress among a group of cowboys who were passing around a jug while they played. The tenderfoot stopped and watched the game for a time, then drifted on to the bar where he ordered a drink. It was about that time that one of the cowboys, who was an epileptic, went off into one of his fits. When the excitement had died down, the stranger started out without drinking his drink. The bartender, who seldom saw a drink go unfinished, demanded to know what was wrong with it.

"I ain't gonna drink it," the newcomer said. "If that's the kind of whiskey you serve, I don't want no part of it."[13]

---

[12] Ramon F. Adams, *Western Words: A Dictionary of the Range, Cow Camp and Trail* (Norman, Okla.: University of Oklahoma Press, 1945), pp. 46-47.

[13] Con Price, *Trails I Rode* (Pasadena, Calif.: Trail's End Publishing Co., 1947), p. 95.

The greener was his favorite play toy

There were times, too, that the cowboy himself was the pilgrim. Every so often a cowboy would accompany a trail drive or a cattle train to some city, and immediately he became the misfit to city ways.

The story is told of the cowboy who checked into a big city hotel, paying $2.50 for his room. He finally conceded to pay such an outlandish price, but when the porter tried to lead him into an elevator he balked.

"No, sir," he said. "I ain't gonna pay $2.50 for no little dinky room such as that."

Jack Potter tells of the time that, as a young boy, he was on his way home from a trail drive and had a layover in Denver:

I followed the crowd down Sixteenth and Curtiss Street and rambled around looking for a quiet place to stop. I found the St. Charles Hotel and made arrangements to stay all night. Then I went off to a barber shop to get my hair cut and clean up a bit. When the barber finished with me he asked if I wanted a bath, and when I said yes, a negro porter took me down the hallway and into a side room. He turned on the water, tossed me a couple of towels and disappeared. I commenced undressing hurriedly, fearing the tub would fill up before I could get ready. The water was within a few inches of the top of the tub when I plunged in. Then I gave a yell like a Comanche Indian, for the water was boiling hot! I came out of the tub on all fours, but when I landed on the marble floor it was so slick that I slipped and fell backwards with my head down. I scrambled around promiscuously, and finally got my footing with a chair for a brace. I thought: "Jack Potter, you are scalded after the fashion of a hog." I caught a lock of my hair to see if it would "slip," at the same time fanning myself with my big Stetson hat. I next examined my toe nails, for they had received a little more dipping than my hair, but I found them in fairly good shape, turning a bit dark, but still hanging on.

That night I went to the Tabor Opera House and saw a fine play. There I found a cowboy chum, and we took in the sights until midnight, when I returned to the St. Charles. The porter showed me up to my room and turned on the gas. When he had gone I undressed to go to bed, and stepped up to blow out the light. I blew and blew until I was out of breath, and then tried to fan the flame out with my hat, but I had to go to bed and leave the gas burning. It was fortunate that I did not succeed, for at that time the papers were full of accounts of people gassed just that way.[14]

---

[14] J. Marvin Hunter (comp, and ed.), *The Trail Drivers of Texas* (2 vols. in 1; Nashville, Tenn.: Cokesbury Press, 1925), pp. 63-64.

Chapter IX

Parlor Sittin'

"Oh, dearest Mary,
What makes you so cruel
When I come to see you
A-riding my mule?"[1]

BEFORE ANYTHING can be said concerning the cowboy as a romantic figure, it is necessary to face the simple fact that the West was not abundant in available females. Lady schoolteachers, sheriff's daughters, female lawyers, and other such

---

[1] Edward Everett Dale, *Cow Country* (Norman, Okla.: University of Oklahoma Press, 1945), p. 152.

pleasantries were as rare as clean socks in a bunk-house. Occasionally a rancher's daughter or a nester girl would blossom forth upon the prairie, but from the scores of cowboys that attended each, only one could win out. And that lucky poke would lose little time in carting off his bride to set up housekeeping on some unclaimed patch of land.

Further, it might be well to point out that most cowboys weren't exactly the gallant Don Juans they are sometimes pictured to be. No real cowboy ever finished a day's work looking or smelling much like a romantic character. And, even dressed and scrubbed to his very best, the cowboy was pretty much aware of his lack of social grace.

One old cowboy was noticed to be giving a great deal of attention to the young son of a certain widow, letting the boy ride with him and becoming real pals with the youngster. When asked why he was doing this, the old poke replied:

"Wal, it's been my experience that when you teach the calf to lead, the old cow will follow."

Another cowboy, newly married, was visiting town with his bride. The papers had recently been full of stories about kidnappers, and the girl was afraid to be left alone in their hotel room. So, when the cowboy left, he locked her in the room, taking the key with him. While making his errands the puncher happened to become involved in a little poker game with some of the boys, and he forgot all about his bride in the hotel room. After several hours he suddenly remembered her and jumped to his feet.

"If there's anything left of me in fifteen minutes, boys," he exclaimed, "I'll be back. But I done left Eda May locked up in a room for twenty-four hours, *an' I ain't neither fed nor watered her!*"[2]

One waddie who was approaching his middle thirties wooed and won a young girl in her late teens. After they were married, the cowboy became the object of a great deal of kidding about sending his wife to school, and so forth. He took it all good-naturedly until, finally, he went away to roundup, taking his wife with him. Several months passed before the cowboy was once again seen on the streets, and a joker asked him how an old stag like him was doing with his cradle robbing.

"Oh, didn't you hear?"

"Hear? About what?"

"About my wife."

---

[2] N. Howard (Jack) Thorp, as told to Neil M. Clark, *Pardner of the Wind* (Caldwell, Idaho: The Caxton Printers, Ltd., 1945), pp. 210-11.

"Why, no. What happened?"

"Wal, it was this way. She was herdin' some mossy-heads inter a draw when her hoss slipped and fell and busted her leg. We buried her right there."

"Buried her? You mean she died of a broken leg?"

"Wal, no. But she was sufferin' so much I jes' couldn't stand it. We had to shoot her."

And the cowboy mosied on down the street, leaving the other to wonder whether or not he had been spoofed.[3]

The cowboy himself was the first to admit his ineptness with women and he told many stories of experiences with them in which his embarrassed awkwardness was evident. Jack Potter, in *The Trail Drivers of Texas,* recalls an incident which occurred as he was riding home on a train after his first trail drive:

At Denison we met up with some immigrant families going to Uvalde, and soon became acquainted with some fine girls in the party. They entertained us all the way down to Taylor, where we changed cars. As we told them good-bye one asked me to write a line in her autograph album.

Now I was sure enough "up a tree." I had been in some pretty tight places and had had to solve some

---

[3] *Ibid.,* pp. 195-96.

pretty hard problems, but this was a new one for me
. . . I begged the young lady to excuse me, but she insisted, so I took the album and began writing down
all the road brands that I was familiar with. But she
told me to write a verse of some kind. I happened to
think of a recitation I had learned at school when I
was a little boy, so I wrote as follows:
"It's tiresome work says lazy Ned, to climb the hill
in my new sled, and beat the other boys. Signed, Your
Bulliest Friend, JACK POTTER."[4]

The story is told about an old rancher who
knew a good deal more about the affairs of the
cow business than those of matrimony. He had
a daughter who was getting a little "long in the
tooth," and he became worried that the girl was
not going to find herself a partner in life.   Finally
the cowman decided to exert a little salesmanship
to help the cause along and he took a prospective
suitor to one side. His recommendation was hon-
est, if not artistic.

"Callie ain't had much eddication," he said,
"but she sure can take a calf by the tail and throw
it over the corral fence."[5]

A cowboy who had just seen a redheaded,
freckled girl whose hair flopped down over her

---

[4] J. Marvin Hunter (comp. and ed.), *The Trail Drivers of Texas*
(2 vols. in 1; Nashville, Tenn.: Cokesbury Press, 1925), pp. 69-70.
[5] Thorp, *op. cit.*, p. 206.

face commented that she reminded him of a steer peeking through a brush fence.

Since pretty girls were so rare on the range, whenever one did drift into a ranch county all the cowboys went mildly berserk. Miss Lillybelle Plunkett arrived in West Texas with her father, who had gone into the cattle business there. Miss Lillybelle was possessed of many charms, none of which was wasted upon the range-riding gentlemen of that section. The cowboys immediately entered into a fierce rivalry to win the girl's affection.

One imaginative poke hit upon the idea of presenting Miss Lillybelle with a gift—a maverick calf on whose rump was branded "L I L." In return he received the supreme pleasure of Lillybelle's company in conversation. But the other cowboys were not to be outdone. They began scouring the range for mavericks, branding each "L I L" and presenting them to the fortunate young lady. Lillybelle was going to have to make a choice, and the cowboys waited anxiously for her decision.

Then one day it came—in the shape of an Eastern tenderfoot whom Lillybelle had known before coming West. She had written and told him of her new prosperity, whereupon he had lost no time in pulling up stakes in her direction with intent to marry. They did—and lived happily on the income from their cattle. No record was made of the language used by the cowboys of West Texas as they rode herd on critters branded "L I L."[6]

Another story is told about the dainty daughter of old man Tom Drake, Texas cattle rancher. The boys came from far and near to court her and, because of her pa's name, they gave cute little Miss Drake the nickname of Duck. She could stand a lot of masculine teasing, and the whole Drake family enjoyed her popularity. But one cowpuncher by the name of Buck Custer became a bit too serious in his wooing of the girl and, on a fine Sunday afternoon, she ordered him to see what was on the other side of the hill —and not to come back.

Buck followed her command, but he swore to revenge himself. He was riding along cursing Miss Drake and the world in general when he suddenly came upon what is known in the cattle areas as a "hatrack," which is an exceedingly bony, tick-covered calf. Buck was inspired. He lifted his lariat rope, twirled his loop, made his catch, and built a fire. Pretty soon he went on his way, his anger somewhat vented.

---

[6] Oren Arnold and John P. Hale, *Hot Irons; Heraldry of the Range* (New York: The Macmillan Company, 1940), p. 52.

*Pretty girls were as rare as clean socks
in the bunkhouse.*

It wasn't long before the Drake brothers discovered the calf, undoubtedly one of the ugliest and scrawniest in Texas, and saw what Buck Custer had done. There upon its side was branded in huge letters, "D U C K."

Some say the Drake boys followed Mr. Custer and branded his hide with numerous bullet holes, while others report that the Drakes were forced to take it out on the hapless calf. All agreed that Buck Custer had made his point.[7]

It was the lack of women on the range that created what is known in cowboy lingo as the "heart-and-hand woman." In 1890 a group of cowboys were killing out the winter months by supplying wood to the army troops stationed at Camp Supply in the Cherokee Outlet. One day, one of the men came back from a trip to Arkansas City with a copy of the matrimonial paper, *The Heart and Hand.* Since this was about the only reading material in camp, outside of can labels which about everybody already had memorized, all the pokes congregated in a tent while John Allen, an Englishman-gone-cowboy, read it aloud.

The paper told about a short road to marriage and how there was a man for every woman and a woman for every man. All you had to do, it

---

[7] *Ibid.,* pp. 52-53.

said, was to write in and you'd get yourself a
mate sent along *pronto*. This excited all the
cowboys because, to be sure, they one and all
wanted to get married—all, that is, except Jim
Pickens who claimed he was a real, first-class
woman-hater.

Everybody else, though, got real excited about
the matter. Tall Cotton, a big cow poke from
Texas, stood up and announced that he thought
it was a crying shame that there were so many
nice girls and widows who wanted to get married
and no good men in sight. Frank Ibaugh said he
agreed and that, for sure, he'd help to save one
from a life of loneliness and misery. Coyote Bill
agreed that he'd help, and a young fellow called
the "Salt Lake Kid," a Mormon from Utah, said
he'd take a half a dozen big, corn-fed gals from
Iowa and Illinois. One waddie declared he would
make a "cowboy-girl" of his, and another stated
that while he didn't know what he'd do with
his, there would be a "doggone big face-licking"
in camp when she arrived.

They all took a vote on the question of getting married, and everybody but Jim Pickens
voted to write for a girl and get spliced. Jim
claimed he would have no part of any such foolish
carryings-on. Everybody got busy picking out
the ad he wanted to answer. They had John

Allen write their letters for them. And it wasn't long before the answers started coming in.

All the girls that answered said they liked cowboys and knew how brave and fearless cowboys were. All of them had about the same story: each had been married to the meanest man alive and had had to leave him, or the other way around. The cowboys agreed on the first day of May as the time set for the girls to arrive. As a preacher was needed from Dodge City, Kansas, a hundred and twenty-five miles away, it was decided that all the women would meet there and all come down together. P. G. Reynolds, of Dodge City, had the only hack line to Camp Supply, and he wanted to charge ten dollars a head to deliver the women. But Ben Nichols, who ran a mule freight line, said he would deliver the goods for five dollars a head and, since the preacher was a Methodist, he would let him ride free of charge.

It was decided that a big farewell bachelor dinner would be held on the fifteenth of April, and a meeting was held to elect officials: referee, master of ceremonies, program chairman, and marshals. Supplies ordered for the party included new tents, blankets, groceries, a thirty-two-gallon barrel of snake medicine, a wagonload of bottled beer, and other articles. Some of the boys thought too much was being spent on groceries and not enough on snake medicine. The committee on arrangements decided that the wives should be entertained with a Wild West show, bronco riding, bullfights, and shooting contests. This would give the women a chance to see what real he-men cowboys they were getting.

The day before the bachelor dinner, all the six-shooters, rifles, butcher knives, and axes were hidden. The dinner was a huge success; even Jim Pickens agreed on that. The cowboys woke up the next morning asking, "How many men did I whip last night?" "Did any of the boys get killed?" "Is there anything wrong with my eyes?" "What's this old rag doing around my head?" "Who owns these boots I got on?" It took a week to get things in good order again.

Two eight-mule teams and six wagons were needed to haul the women and their baggage from Dodge City. When they drove into camp and began to crawl out of the wagons, the cowboys were all falling over one another hunting up the ones that answered to their names as the preacher called them out. Eight girls failed to show up and, when the name matching was over, there was a big, fat widow with six kids left over. It was clear that she had tagged along just to take potluck, but nobody seemed to care very much. The cowboys talked it over and decided that the only thing to do was to put her up as first prize in the Wild West show.

Jim Pickens had been standing to one side while all the shouting was going on but, when it was time for the Wild West show to start, he stepped up and entered. He said he didn't want any prize, that he just wanted to prove to one and all that he was the best cowboy in the Cherokee Strip. And sure enough he was. He won all the roping, the bronco riding, and the shooting contests. And when it was all over and he was the winner, all the other cow pokes agreed that he was bound to accept the prize he had won. They made him stand up and get hitched to the widow with the six kids.[8]

Another term applied to these women, more specifically to homely women, was "Montgomery Ward women sent West on approval." A typical range remark following such a marriage was, "I hear old Ike Jones over at the Lazy J got himself hitched up. Don't know who she is . . . reckon he musta got her from Monkey Ward!"[9]

And there is a story of one cowboy who fell

---

[8] John James Callison, *Bill Jones of Paradise Valley, Oklahoma; His Life and Adventures for Over Forty Years in the Great Southwest* (Chicago, Printed by M. A. Donohue & Co. [c. 1914]), pp. 90-101.

[9] Philip Ashton Rollins, *The Cowboy, His Characteristics, His Equipment, and His Part in the Development of the West* (Reprint ed.; New York: Charles Scribner's Sons, 1936), p. 170.

for a picture of a girl in a mail-order catalogue
(shepherd's bible). Thinking that everything in
it was for sale, he ordered one of the models for
a wife, fluffy dress and all. Then he bragged to
other pokes that it wouldn't cost him anything
because the company sent everything postpaid.[10]

Perhaps it was the cowboy's disappointments
in such affairs that caused him to be extremely
skeptical of marriage. As goes the toast once re-
cited by a cowboy at a wedding:

> A wedding is the greatest place
> For folks to go and learn.
> He thought that she was his'n
> But found that he was her'n.[11]

Jim Collins, of the Half Circle H, once went
to a wedding in company with another puncher.
The bride was the young daughter of an old
nester, and the groom a gangling granger boy.
Jim sat silently through the ceremony until the
minister came to the part about, "With all my
worldly goods I thee endow." When the groom
had repeated the promise, Jim nudged his companion and whispered:

---

[10] Ramon F. Adams, *Western Words: A Dictionary of the Range,
Cow Camp and Trail* (Norman, Okla.: University of Oklahoma
Press, 1945), p. 142.

[11] Arnold and Hale, *op. cit.*, p. 217.

"There goes Sam's shotgun. Somebody stole his dog just last week."[12]

A drunk cowboy one night asked a girl to dance with him and was refused. He promptly told her where to go. The girl's brother was at the dance, and she informed him of the insult which had been directed at her. The brother caught the waddie and insisted that he apologize to the girl. The brother was big, and the cowboy wasn't *that* drunk. He promised to make the apology.

"I take it all back," he told the girl when he found her. "You don't need to go to the devil after all. Your brother 'n me has made other arrangements!"[13]

A cowboy was visiting a friend who had recently married and was having mother-in-law troubles. The cowboy suggested to the fellow that they go out and drown his sorrows.

"It wouldn't work," the friend said disconsolately. "She can swim!"

In Cheyenne, once, a hefty son of the range became so enthralled at the coyote-tremolo rendition by a blonde soprano of "The Last Kiss My Darling Mother Gave" that he hurled a twenty-

---

[12] Dale, *op. cit.*, p. 144.
[13] *Ibid.*, p. 145.

dollar gold piece in her direction. It hit her behind the ear and knocked her senseless.[14]

Another Western town was visited by a traveling show troupe which included a concert singer. One cowboy was urging a buddy to go with him.

"Is she any good?" he was asked.

"Good? Why, man, she's a virtuoso!"

"To heck with her morals," the waddie snorted. "I want to know if she can sing."[15]

Tollie Sands was supposed to be the homeliest man, without exception, in the Guadalupe Mountains of New Mexico, but, nevertheless, his wife Eliza was extremely jealous of a widow lady in town whom she thought to be after Tollie. So the story goes, a peddler one day stopped at their ranch and showed Tollie a mirror, something he had never seen or heard of before. He liked what he saw in it and asked, "How much for this picture?" He paid the price and kept it.

Later, Eliza, who had been away gathering wood at the time, was snooping in Tollie's things and came across the mirror. "So *that's* the sour-faced

---

[14] Rollins, *op. cit.*, pp. 322-23.

[15] C. K. Stillwagon, *Rope Chokers; A Collection of Human Interest Stories, Anecdotes, Historical Fragments, and Pictures of the Oil Fields* (Houston, Tex.: Well Equipment Mfg. Co., 1945), p. 127.

old hussy you've been chasin' is it!" she said, and smashed the mirror over Tollie's head.[16]

Like Eliza, cowboys looked upon the vows of betrothal as serious matters. One Texas cowboy was engaged to a little girl who made a visit to the big city. While there she wrote to the cowboy, telling him of the wonderful time she was having and mentioning the modern marvel of having a hotel room with running water. It was but a short time before she received a wire from the cowboy. It read:

"Get rid of that Indian at once or our engagement is off."[17]

One old bachelor, a wealthy rancher, had a sister who lived in the big city and who was constantly harping at him to let her show him the town. The old boy didn't care much for cities, but the day came when he had a load of cattle headed in that direction. He gave in and wired his sister that he was on his way. The sister was anxious to show him a good time and had things all arranged, with dinner at a downtown hotel and a show scheduled for later. The lady whom the sister had chosen for him was the middle-

---

[16] Thorp, *op. cit.*, p. 209.

[17] Frank M. King, *Wranglin' the Past* (Pasadena, Calif.: Trail's End Publishing Co., 1935), p. 88.

aged, gushing type, and the old cowman didn't care much for her. After dinner, it was decided that they would walk the three or four blocks to the theater.

As they left the hotel, the cowman managed to slip a chew of tobacco into his mouth, and he and the lady friend followed along behind the others. The cowman's companion chattered away about the social life in the city, letting him know she was on the "in" with those who amounted to something around town. Finally, she got to what was strongest on her mind.

"I understand that you own an enauhmous ranch and just oodles of cows."

The wealthy cattleman shifted his tobacco expertly in his jaw and replied solemnly:

"Wal, ma'am, I don't reely *own* all thet, but I'm cookin' fer one of the biggest outfits in Texas."[18]

The cowboy that got married was an exception to the rule. For the most part he belonged to a womanless world. For the girl who married a cowboy, there was generally a hard, lonely life ahead. But divorces were scarce, unless, that is, you were in Judge Roy Bean's territory. Roy defended his right to grant divorces this way:

---

[18] Dale, *op. cit.*, pp. 144-45.

"Heck, I married 'em, didn't I? Then I got the right to un-marry 'em. A man has the right to rectify his own errors, ain't he?"[19]

---

[19] Based on a story told by C. L. Sonnichsen in *Roy Bean; Law West of the Pecos* (New York: The Macmillan Company, 1943), p. 114.

Chapter X

Next Year's Savings

"When I got to the boss
And tried to draw my roll,
He had me figured out
Nine dollars in the hole.[1]

ONE OF THE more admirable characteristics of the cowboy was his attitude toward material wealth. Few cowboys ever owned much more than their horse, saddle, six gun, and a change of clothing,

---

[1] From the cowboy song, "The Chisholm Trail," as quoted by William Elsey Connelley in his *Wild Bill and His Era; The Life & Adventures of James Butler Hickok* (New York: The Press of the Pioneers, 1933), p. 149.

and few of them ever really expected to have much more than that at any time in their lives. The early West was a poor man's home and the primary reward of being a cowboy was the pleasure of living a cowboy's existence. Ramon F. Adams says of the cowboy:

> Unlike us, to him money meant nothing. He would work hard for thirty dollars a month, then spend it all with his characteristic freeheartedness in an hour of relaxation. All he was seriously concerned about was plenty to eat, a good horse to ride, a saddle for his throne, and he was King.[2]

This attitude was instrumental in the creation of what was known as the "range code" which allowed ranch folks to trustingly leave their doors unlocked when away from home. It was an accepted custom for a cowboy to stop at an unattended ranch house, enter, and help himself to the food. All that was expected of him was that he clean up his mess before he left.

Cowboys often referred to their personal belongings as their "trinkets" or "plunder." Agnes Morley Cleaveland, in *No Life for a Lady*, tells of a cowboy who stopped at her ranch on his way to a local roundup. While he was eating, some-

---

[2] Ramon F. Adams, *Cowboy Lingo* (Boston: Houghton Mifflin Company, 1936), p. 149.

thing stampeded his string of horses, and with them went the pack horse carrying his bedroll. The man leaped from his chair shouting, "There goes the savin's of a lifetime!"[3]

One cowboy was drinking at a bar when his boss came up and told him that he had been raised in pay an extra ten dollars a month.

"Th' heck!" said the cowboy. "I haven't even drunk up last month's pay yet. That extra ten dollars'll kill me fer sure!"[4]

Another cowboy had been in town all weekend and was in the bunkhouse telling the boys about it.

"I went to town with fifty dollars," he said, "and now I ain't got one red cent of it."

"Gosh," someone said. "What did you do with all of it?"

"Wal, first off I mosied into a saloon. I goes up to the bar and yells that I'll buy the drinks for the house. The house takes me up on it for ten dollars worth. Then I trots down to another saloon and do the same thing all over ag'in. This time it cost me fifteen dollars. By now I 'uz

---

[3] Agnes Morley Cleaveland in *No Life for a Lady* (Boston: Houghton Mifflin Company, 1941), as quoted by Ramon F. Adams in *Western Words* (Norman, Okla.: University of Oklahoma Press, 1945), p. 164.

[4] Willie Newbury Lewis, *Between Sun and Sod* (Clarendon, Tex.: Clarendon Press, 1938), p. 120.

feelin' my appetite stirrin' around, so I goes to a restaurant and orders me a ten-dollar meal. So this morning I'm plumb broke."

"Yes, but ten and ten is twenty, an' fifteen is only thirty-five dollars. What do you think you did with the rest of your fifty dollars?"

The cowboy scratched his head thoughtfully. "Derned if I know, boys. I musta spent that other fifteen dollars foolishly!"[5]

The cowman who started a brand called "%" ("Per cent") had strong hopes of having his investment pay off. However, that was not the case and, with cattle country irony, he changed the brand to "00" ("Double Zero").[6]

Walter Billingsley, a well-known Texas trail driver, likes to tell of the time he drove a herd of Texas beef to Wyoming for the King Ranch. Everything went along fine until they reached a trail town in Nebraska where they stopped for a short rest. Naturally the boys wanted to clean up and take in the town. This was all fine and good, but five of them had had enough of trail driving and did not report back for work. Billingsley rode to town the next morning, found

---

[5] Edward Everett Dale, *Cow Country* (Norman, Okla.: University of Oklahoma Press, 1945), p. 140.

[6] Oren Arnold and John P. Hale, *Hot Irons; Heraldry of the Range* (New York: The Macmillan Company, 1940), p. 63.

the boys, and fired them on the spot. It was then that he realized he owed the men a considerable hunk of wages and did not have a red cent on him.

He went to see the town's banker and explained that he was trail bossing a King's Ranch herd and that he wished to cash a check. But when the banker asked for identification, Billingsley had none. The banker suggested that the trail boss look around town to see if he could find someone to identify him. The Texan looked but found no one he knew. Then an idea hit him, and he rode for camp.

That afternoon the banker heard a rumble of hoofs, and then someone called for him to come outside. It was Billingsley. And with him he had brought his entire *remuda* and the chuck wagon pulled by six mules. All of them carried the K W brand.

"I guess you know what the King Ranch brand is, don't you?" Billingsley said. "I reckon this ought to give you plenty of identification."

The banker agreed and with a big grin, cashed the check for Billingsley.[7]

Con Price tells the story of old Dan Sullivan who made a lot of money on a horse herd and

[7] J. Frank Dobie, *On the Open Range* (Dallas, Tex.: Southwest Press, 1931), pp. 169-71.

retired from his cowboy life to open and manage
a hotel in a cow town. Dan knew every puncher
for miles around—and they knew him. During
the winter months when jobs were scarce, nearly
a dozen waddies drifted in to spend the winter
with him. Of course they were dead broke, but
Dan just couldn't bring himself to throw them
out, even when they practically ate and drank
him into bankruptcy.[8]

But even the generous soul of the cowboy could
be overtouched. Jake Saunders was hit up by
an old range dog for a loan of twenty dollars.
Saunders knew that the man had a reputation
for borrowing and gave him only ten dollars.

"I asked for twenty," the man complained.

"That's all right," Jake answered. "We're even.
You've lost ten, and I've lost ten."[9]

Chronic borrowers were, in fact, none too pop-
ular on the range. Old Tom Mews was one, and
the boys of his outfit had long since learned to
control their generosity with him. One day, however, Tom went to sleep in the branding pen
after working hours. As he slept a calf came
up and, tasting the crusted salt in his breeches,

---

[8] Con Price, *Trails I Rode* (Pasadena, Calif.: Trail's End Publishing Co., 1947), pp. 191-92.

[9] Philip Ashton Rollins, *The Cowboy, His Characteristics, His
Equipment and His Part in the Development of the West* (Reprint ed.; New York: Charles Scribner's Sons, 1936), p. 76.

*He'd risk his month's wages on the
turn of a card.*

ate his pants almost completely off. Naturally Tom had been too tight to bring along an extra pair as the other cowboys had done, and he tried to borrow some from them. But not a one would help him out. Tom finally had to ride to town to buy a new pair—with his skinny old legs bare to the world.[10]

A cowboy who had a reputation like that of Tom was on roundup and asked the cook to get him some tobacco on his trip to town. He had nothing less than a twenty-dollar bill, and he grudgingly handed it over to the cookie. When the dough-belly returned, the first thing the cowboy asked for was his change.

"Change?" said the cook. "You didn't say nothin' about change. I supposed you wanted to pay back what you've been borryin'."

And he dumped out *twenty dollars' worth of Duke's Mixture* at the cowboy's feet![11]

It may seem strange that the cowboy should work long and hard for months, then throw his earnings away in one wild night of spending. Yet such a recklessness with his fortune was the cowboy's way.

---

[10] N. Howard (Jack) Thorp, as told to Neil M. Clark, *Pardner of the Wind* (Caldwell, Idaho: The Caxton Printers, Ltd., 1945), p. 204.

[11] *Ibid.*, p. 204.

The feeling experienced on a trip to town is very well illustrated in J. L. McCaleb's story of hitting Abilene, Kansas, after a long trail drive.

. . . We went into town, tied our ponies, and the first place we visited was a saloon and dance hall. We ordered toddies like we had seen older men do, and drank them down, for we were dry, very dry, as it had been a long way between drinks. I quit my partner, as he had a girl to talk to, so I went out and in a very short time I went into another store and saloon. I got another toddy, my hat began to stiffen up, but I pushed it up in front, moved my pistol to where it would be handy, then sat down on a box in the saloon and picked up a newspaper and thought I would read a few lines, but my two toddies were at war, so I could not very well understand what I read. I got up and left for more sights. . . . I headed for a place across the street, where I could hear a fiddle. It was a saloon, gambling and dance hall. Here I saw an old, long-haired fellow dealing monte. I went to the bar and called for a toddy, and as I was drinking it a girl came up and put her little hand under my chin, and looked me square in the face and said, "Oh, you pretty Texas boy, give me a drink." I asked her what she wanted and she said anything I took, so I called for two toddies. My, I was getting rich fast—a pretty girl and plenty of whiskey. My old hat was now away back on my head. My boss had given me four dollars spending money and I had my five-dollar bill, so I told the girl that she could make herself easy; that I was going to break the monte game, buy out the saloon, and keep her to run it for me when I went back to Texas for my other herd of cattle. Well, I went to the old, long-haired dealer, and as he was making a new layout I put my five on the first card (a king) and about the third pull I won. I now had ten dollars and I thought I had better go and get another toddy before I played again. As I was getting rich so fast, I put the two bills on the tray and won. Had now twenty dollars, so I moved my hat back as far as it would go and went to get a drink—another toddy, but my girl was gone. I wanted to show her that I was not joking about buying out the saloon after I broke the bank. After this drink things did not look so good. I went back and it seemed to me that I did not care whether I broke him or not. I soon lost all I had won and my old original five. When I quit him my hat was becoming more settled, getting more down in front, and I went out, found my partner and left for camp. The next morning, in place of owning a saloon and going back to Texas after my other herds, I felt—oh! what's the use? You old fellows know how I felt.[12]

The West's love for gambling, the willingness to risk all on the turn of a card, found humorous expression in verse:

'T was midnight in the faro bank,
Faces pale and cheeks aglow,
A score of sports were gathered,
Watching fortune's ebb and flow.

There was one who saw the last turn
With eyes of deep dismay,
And, as the Queen slipped from the box,
Cried, "Broke!" and turned away.

---

[12] J. Marvin Hunter (comp. and ed.), *The Trail Drivers of Texas* (2 vols. in 1; Nashville, Tenn.: Cokesbury Press, 1925), pp. 486-87.

For a moment on the table
Down his throbbing head he laid,
Then, looking 'round him wildly,
He clenched his hand and said:

"I'm a pretty slick young feller,
I've been given every deal,
Have often dropped my bankroll,
But was never known to squeal.

"But this evening I am weary,
And my socks are hanging low,
My usual gait is 2:13
But tonight I'm trotting slow.

" 'T is not for myself I'm kicking,
I've a friend that's near and dear
Who is lying, worn with sickness,
A couple of blocks from here.

"She's my darling, gents, my darling,
But they say she's got to croak,
And the medicine to save her
I can't get—you see I'm broke."

"Here's a dollar," said the dealer.
A smile lit up his face,
"Thanks, old man,—damn the medicine,
I'll play it on the ace!"[18]

A cowboy went into a mercantile store to buy some personal effects. When he had rounded up what he wanted, he told the proprietor that he

---

[18] Duncan Emrich, *It's an Old Wild West Custom* (New York: Vanguard Press, Inc., 1949), p. 88. Reprinted by permission.

would have to pay so much cash and give him a "slow note," meaning it would be some time before he could pay for the rest. When he had gone, the storekeeper scratched his head and wondered just how slow a slow note was.

One cowboy, a man with a good deal of Scotch blood in his veins, supposedly went into a store and purchased a spur—only one. When asked why he didn't buy the spur for his other foot, the cowboy answered that he was under the impression that as long as one side of the horse moved, so would the other. And he could see no sense in wasting money by buying two spurs.

In the Oklahoma Osage country an Indian was said to have walked into a bank and asked for a sizeable loan. The banker inquired as to what security the Indian had.

"Me gottum five hundred horses," replied the Indian.

The banker checked on this and found it to be true, so he made the loan. Some time later the Indian returned to the bank with a huge roll of bills in his hand and paid off his note. The banker, noting how much the Indian had left, suggested to him that he let the bank take care of it for him. The Indian looked suspiciously at the banker.

"How many horses you gottum?" he asked.[14]

Not all cowboys were above their moments of greed, of course. Bank raids, train holdups, and stagecoach robberies were undertaken for more than just sport. Yet, even the outlaws often felt a touch of the Robin Hood spirit.

An outlaw was busy sticking up a train one afternoon when he came to an old fellow who shook his head and said:

"I'm sorry, but I have nothing to give you."

The outlaw looked at him suspiciously.

"How come? Who are you?"

"My name is Reverend Appleton. I am a Methodist minister."

The outlaw scratched the back of his neck with his six gun, then dropped a big handful of coins into the minister's lap.

"Here," he said. "You take this. I'm a Methodist, too."[15]

In similar vein, Curley Bill once attended church and forced the congregation to sing hymns for several hours. Then he passed the collection

---

[14] C. K. Stillwagon, *Rope Chokers: A Collection of Human Interest Stories, Anecdotes, Historical Fragments, and Pictures of the Oil Fields* (Houston, Tex.: Well Equipment Mfg. Co., 1945), p. 109.

[15] Eric Thane [R. C. Henry], *High Border Country* (New York: Duell, Sloan and Pearce, 1942), p. 182.

plate with a pistol in one hand and took up the largest amount in the history of the church.

In fact, it was nothing particularly unusual for a gunman, after adding a new notch or two to the butt of his gun, to attempt to square things by attending church and dropping a sack of gold dust into the collection plate.

There is a story that Parson Tom Uzzell once preached in a gambling house in Creed. When the hat was passed a good collection was taken, but it wasn't good enough to satisfy Bat Masterson. That night some of the boys crept into the parson's hotel room and stole his breeches. When Parson Tom discovered his pants missing, he stormed down into the saloon lobby in his long handles.

Strangely, none of the boys seemed to know a thing about the parson's pants, so finally Tom enlisted the aid of the law and returned to his room. There, hanging on the foot of the bed, was the missing clothing. Only now the pockets were jammed with currency and silver.[16]

Despite her moments of violence and greed, the Old West was an "open-doored" West which honored the values of hospitality and generosity

---

[16] William MacLeod Raine, *Guns on the Frontier; The Story of How Law Came to the West* (Cleveland: World Publishing Co., 1940), pp. 252-53.

and respected the honesty of men. The value of a man's personal integrity was fundamental in the makeup of the American cowboy. Nowhere is it more obvious than in the freehearted, wholesome laughter of the range.